# MAHATMA GANDHI AND COMPARATIVE RELIGION

*By the Same Author*

The Concept of *Śraddhā*

Mahatma Gandhi and C. F. Andrews: A Study in Hindu-Christian Dialogue

# MAHATMA GANDHI
## AND
# COMPARATIVE RELIGION



K. L. SESHAGIRI RAO

MOTILAL BANARSIDASS
Delhi :: Varanasi :: Patna

MOTILAL BANARSIDASS
Indological Publishers and Booksellers
*Head Office*: BUNGALOW ROAD, JAWAHAR NAGAR, DELHI-7
*Branches* : I. CHOWK, VARANASI-I (U.P.)
2. ASHOK RAJPATH, PATNA-4 (BIHAR)



*First Edition* : *Delhi*, 1978

Printed in India
BY SHANTILAL JAIN AT SHRI JAINENDRA PRESS, A-45, PHASE-I, INDUSTRIAL AREA, NARAINA, NEW DELHI-28 AND PUBLISHED BY NARENDRA PRAKASH JAIN, FOR MOTILAL BANARSIDASS, BUNGALOW ROAD, JAWAHAR NAGAR, DELHI-7

CONTENTS

# FOREWORD

Very few have written adequately about Gandhi's religious beliefs and attitudes and his spiritual life. In fact, Gandhi himself has written about them only casually and incidentally. He never tried to deal with them in a systematic manner. The reason is obvious. His constant endeavor to act and practice spirituality and religion, according to his own light rather than preach them, urged him to take headlong to the field of action. His tireless activities and efforts at significant achievements in the political field, his endeavors for revolutionary reforms in the social sphere, his initiation of new ideas in the economics of his own country, and his fresh orientation in education left him no time even to complete his own well begun autobiography. It stops at 1921; it is with a "wrench" that he takes leave of his expectant readers at that point.

This suspension, though a substantial gain to the Indian historical scene for the next thirty-seven years, means a serious loss to the important subject of hagiology and the mystical literature of the world. Never has so saintly and spiritual a person engaged himself so constantly (with equal zest and attention) in such mundane matters, all the way from a fight for political freedom down to the cleaning of a latrine. How could we expect so busy and action-oriented a person to write a full treatise on his own religion and spirituality ? How could he give us a complete picture of his inner life except in a few glimpses ? And yet it is clear from his own declaration that his one aim in life was "self-realization, to see God face to face, to attain Moksha" — Salvation.

There can be no doubt that Gandhi's deep faith in God and his general spiritual outlook were the source of his almost inexhaustible intellectual and emotional energy, of his confidence in the essential goodness of human beings, of his fearless abandon in conducting what he called his experiments with Truth, and the charismatic influence he wielded on the leaders and masses of India for well-nigh three decades. On November 26, 1925, he wrote, "I should certainly like to narrate my experiments in the spiritual field which are only known to myself and from which I have derived such power as I possess for working in the political field" — and in other fields as well. In fact, a constant and steady spirituality was the fountainhead of his strength and power in everything that he said and did. No one who had not anchored himself in spirituality could have dared challenge "sword-force" by "soul-force", naked violence by non-violence. Spirituality is the basis of all religions; the essence of religion, as Gandhi put it, is morality, and morality is truthfulness in thought, word, and deed.

Gandhi's search for Truth, the quest of Being in the Becoming, the ceaseless efforts to realize the Transcendent Reality as immanent in the world in which we live and move and have our being, was itself religious in its origin and intensity, as well as eminently pragmatic and practical in its purpose.

Gandhi started with the faith as well as conviction that God is Truth; to him the lustre and "mighty effulgence of Truth" was million times more intense than that of the physical sun. As early as 1925, he wrote, "My uniform experience had convinced me that there is no other God than Truth." Later he declared that "Truth is God." He said, "God is denied by man," but there is yet to be born a person who can deny Truth as he has perceived it, to which his whole being has been a witness. Seldom has there been a life lived with such earnestness and utter commitment to the Truth one has oneself perceived, from day to day, as that of Gandhi's.

But Gandhi does not stop with the statement that the attainment and realization of Truth in his own life and action is his sole end and aim. He adds, with equal if not greater emphasis, that for him the only means of attaining Truth in life is Ahiṁsā — Non-violence — Love. In bidding farewell to his readers in his *Autobiography* he says that for him "the only means for the realization of Truth is Ahiṁsā."

Gandhi makes it clear that "a perfect vision of Truth can only follow a complete realization of Ahiṁsā." Moreover, Ahiṁsā-Nonviolence-Love is nothing less than "the ability to love the meanest of creation as oneself." He further says, that such utter loving identification with everything that lives is impossible without self-purification, that is to say, self transcendence. To be utterly selfless and passion-free in thought, word, and deed (the triple purity) is the very essence of self-transcendence.

Real love springs forth spontaneously from such purification.

The study of the life, thought, and action of Gandhi from the religious point of view is extremely interesting. The most remarkable aspect of such a study is its revelation of an unbreakable and sequential chain beginning with his spiritual insight about the existence of one Supreme Power, through his religious belief in an ever-responding God, on to his declaration that Truth itself is God and that the attainment of Truth is possible, so far as he was concerned, only through love, service, and sacrifice, shorn of all self, and that that again can result only from purity and self-transcendence. Gandhi does not stop at knowing and understanding Truth; he must proceed to establish the same in terms of justice and fair play to all — but always and without exception by and through Non-violence.

It is in this unique way that Gandhi brings home to everyone the religious spirit — not in heavy theological language but in the language of daily life and truthful living.

Gandhi was frankly a religious Hindu and a *Sanātani* Hindu at that. He was relentless, however, in his criticism of the excrescences that had accumulated in Hinduism through the ages. He was equally active in campaigning for their removal. Two persons as different as Jawaharlal Nehru and C. F. Andrews have testified to the fact that Hinduism was the root and stem of his religious life. Gandhi however was always generous in acknowledging his deep debt to other faiths.

His attitude toward other religions could be said to be that of the ancient Vedic rishis who sang, "let noble thoughts come to us from every side." But he said that while we should throw open our windows for fresh breezes to blow through our halls, we should refuse to be swept off our feet. His attitude may also be likened to that of the Asokan Edict which declares, *samavāya eva sādhu*, concord alone is the best of attitudes in matters of religion; we understand our own religion better by studying other religions with an open mind.

Gandhi was never dogmatic in religious matters nor did he ever try to persuade others that Hinduism was the greatest or the highest of all religions. He was not an eclectic either, in the sense of picking up good things from different religions and then weaving a pattern of his own. He was neither syncretic nor synthetic in his approach. "I am a man of religion," he would say, but he would add, "I believe in the Religion of Religions." God has given man two instruments, reason and morality. Gandhi held that all things that parade in the name of religion should be tested by these two instruments. But he would add that he who wants to test them must himself be pure and devoid of all selfish taint.

Gandhi's attitude may be described as pluralistic in religion, but with an important and an essential proviso, namely, that there should be equal respect on the part of each religion for the others. No historical religion is perfect or can be perfect; but each religion has enough Truth in it to suffice for its followers to work out their own salvation. At the same time, no religion should bar its followers from the study of other religions to supplement their own knowledge and spiritual discipline.

Broadly speaking, Gandhi's approach is in essence humanistic. All religions come into being to supply the spiritual needs of the people amongst whom they have taken root. No religion can be said to retain today its pristine purity as at its birth. In the very nature of things, change and evolution are the law of life; religion is no exception. Since communication and contact have become world-wide, people belonging to different religions and various environments mingle together in pursuit of their various activities. The Gandhian call for mutual respect among religious people of different persuasions, without any sense of superiority or inferiority seems to be the most rational and feasible, if they are to benefit from each other.

Gandhi held strong views against proselytization, consistent with his general view about religion. While real conversion, which is spiritual in essence, cannot be taken exception to, he strongly objected to mere quantitative proselytization.

From the very beginning of his public career in South Africa and later in India, he always came in contact with people of different religions and creeds. At all times, it was his good fortune to have had either as colleagues or as followers persons of different faiths. Two striking examples are those of Moulana Abdul Kalam Azad, who was a devout Muslim, and Rev. C. F. Andrews who was not only a Christian but a missionary. This was possible on account of Gandhi's catholic attitude, and his rational as well as liberal views about religion and the relationship between different religions. As is well known, his Ashram prayers derived from all religions, and became a daily feature in his Ashram and wherever he went. This healthy tradition still continues in Vinoba's Paunar Ashram and other Gandhian Ashrams all over India.

In India, Gandhi befriended the Muslims, as early as 1921, by identifying himself with the Khilafat cause. It seemed that Hindu-Muslim unity, despite the attempt of the foreign rulers to divide them, would become an accomplished fact. But political considerations dashed these hopes to the ground and led to the tragic partition of the country, which Gandhi deeply regretted.

From many points of view, the present study of Mahatma Gandhi's spiritual unfoldment and religious beliefs and views is illuminating and valuable. The treatment breaks new ground and opens a vista which provokes further study of Gandhi's spiritual life. It takes not only a comprehensive view but is comparative in its approach. The study shows how one whose whole life was cast in a religious mould looked upon other religions and could work in common with people of different religions in amity and concordance, despite certain important differences. The Muslims, for instance, have strong views about image-worship as practiced by Hindus and about their protection of the cow. The Christians differ from the Hindus in matters of conversion. The author has covered every important aspect of religion and has specially referred to Truth and Non-violence, which were Gandhi's guiding stars in all matters. In fact, one could say that "Truth through Non-violence alone," is his whole religious creed.

The treatment of such an important subject as spirituality and religion, that too in connection with a world figure like Gandhi required a background of deep and comprehensive study. A comparative study was still more difficult. Dr. K. L. Seshagiri Rao has a record of serious religious study for years, and possesses the essential background in Comparative Religion through his training at the Center for the Study of World Religions at Harvard University. He has himself a profound sense of religion and spirituality in addition to his scholarship.

*The Gandhi Bibliography* published by the Gandhi Peace Foundation in New Delhi, contains five hundred and thirty-six dispersed references to Gandhi's religion and spirituality. But no detailed or systematic treatment is available in any one volume.

I know of only three limited studies of Gandhi's religion and spirituality. One is by Professor Narayana Rao A. Nikam, another by Dr. R. D. Ranade, and the third by myself. But none of them can be said to approach anywhere near the very logical, comprehensive and comparative study covering the various aspects of the subject which we find in the present volume.

Everything that Gandhi said, did, or wrote bears witness to his faith in Truth, God, and Spirituality. The publication of this study fills a long-felt need for better understanding of Gandhi not only as a religious man and a spiritual seeker but as a constructive promoter of harmony and mutual respect among religions.

R. R. Diwakar
*Chairman*,
Gandhi Peace Foundation,

New Delhi
February 8, 1978

# PREFACE

My involvement in Gandhian studies is both academic and existential. It received a sharp focus during 1960-62 when I worked with the Gandhi Peace Foundation, New Delhi, as a Research Fellow. It was Gandhi's religious thought and concerns that particularly engaged my attention; they proved to be a vast and fertile area of investigation. Ever since, I have been carrying on research on selected topics in this area as I could find the time.

In my early essay entitled *Mahtma Gandhi and C. F. Andrews: A Study in Hindu-Christian Dialogue*, I dealt with the problems and promises of Hindu-Christian relations as revealed in the great friendship of these two towering personalities of twentieth-century India. The present work, *Mahatma Gandhi and Comparative Religion*, traces Gandhi's own religious development and focuses on his study of and approach to the major world religions. I hope to follow it by another work in this general field: *Mahatma Gandhi and Khan Abdul Gaffar Khan: A Study in Hindu-Islamic Dialogue.*

For the preparation of this work, I owe more than I can ever express or assess to the writings of Mahatma Gandhi. I am indebted to my esteemed friend, the poet and author John Moffitt, who read these pages and from whose criticisms and encouragement I have benefited. To Sri. R. R. Diwakar, Chairman, Gandhi Peace Foundation, I also express my gratitude for his gracious *Foreword.* I thank those whose writings I have referred in this book.

This work is dedicated with faith and hope to the cause of inter-religious harmony in India.

Charlottesville, Va.
August 15, 1978

K. L. Seshagiri Rao
*University of Virginia*

# INTRODUCTION

The study of comparative religion is one of the most important enterprises of our time. Of all the factors that account for the peculiar shape of a culture and the outlook of its people upon themselves and upon the world around them, religion must be taken as among the most primary. It occupies an important place in almost every age and society in human history down to the present. It relates to the wellsprings of individual and social life and raises central questions regarding human life and destiny. Religion is an extraordinarily interesting side of humanity, and one neglects it at the risk of failing to understand human life, society, and history.

Gandhi believed that education without the study of religions is incomplete. Religion, in its varied forms, is not only a legitimate intellectual pursuit but a vital aspect of human culture and civilization. Reminiscing about his early life, Gandhi regretted very much the lack of facilities to study religion at school. But he made this up later by devoting a good measure of his time and energy to the study of comparative religion. This study exercised a profound impact on the course of his life. In the first chapter of the present work, I have discussed the diverse religious influences that shaped Gandhi's life.

The study of religions, for Gandhi, was not a purely theoretical or academic matter; it was also a practical and existential necessity. He was, therefore, interested in living religions, not dead ones. Whether in England or South Africa or India, he was invariably involved with the question of religious diversity and the problem of forging unity among the followers of different religions through inter-religious understanding. His own life was dedicated to the search for Truth, and the different ways through which human beings pursued Truth interested him exceedingly. And in the course of his "experiments with Truth," he developed an enlightened and constructive approach to the study of all religions. The second chapter analyzes his critical and constructive study of four major, living religions with which he was confronted, namely, Hinduism, Buddhism, Christianity, and Islam.

The lack of sensitive understanding of one another's faith has often led the practitioners of religions to mutual recrimination and even bloodshed. People quarrel about religion when they lose sight of the human dimension of all religions. This situation is, in no small measure, due to the fact that religious believers have generally insufficient opportunities for and interest in knowing about the values and insights in world religions; indeed, there is pervasive ignorance of the creative principles of all faiths. Whatever the reason for such a state of affairs in the past, Gandhi felt that it cannot be allowed to continue. Modern men and women need to expand their religious consciousness by understanding in depth the spiritual truths revealed in other faiths. Gandhi's own study of the fundamentals of different religions made him better understand his fellow men and women and enabled him to develop a universal and integrated view of religion and its significance in the history of humanity. This theme is explored in the chapter entitled "Principles of Creative Religion."

The study of comparative religion enabled Gandhi to cooperate with the followers of other religions in realizing the higher ideals of life. It showed that all religions have a common objective, namely, the disciplining of human beings so that they may attain self transcendence and fulfillment. He discovered for himself that all religions have elements of truth, and none is in exclusive possession of the whole truth. Therefore, he accepted all great religions as necessary and essentially true. He considered the uniqueness of each religious tradition as something precious, and therefore, to be cherished by the followers of all religions. He believed that the study of religions would contribute to healthy religious pluralism, which would respect genuine religious differences. In this connection, he formulated the concept of "reverence for *dharma*", which is expanded in the chapter on "Inter-religious Relations."

Gandhi reflected deeply on some persisting problems of all religions and suggested ways and means of dealing with them. These have been discussed in a separate chapter. And the last chapter presents the conclusions of the study.

CHAPTER 1

# SPIRITUAL UNFOLDMENT OF GANDHI

NO thinker in modern times has perhaps experienced so keen a struggle within himself regarding the momentous issues of religious faith as has Mahatma Gandhi. His whole life was one unceasing quest for anchorage of faith in a "living God." His was a personality in which the deepest strand was the religious. It was the religious motivation that made his life a compelling example and the center of attention of people throughout the world. For him the best kind of life was the life of good deeds and selfless service to humanity. Though he did not yield himself to the persistent efforts made to convert him to a religion other than his own, he could incorporate the insights of other religions into his in an endeavor to realize the inner truths of all religions. Faith and reason, the spiritual and the ethical, had so blended in him that he was able to steer clear of the irrational superstitions that smother what is of inestimable value in religion.

Further, though he opened his mind to the powerful influences of modern thought currents, he never gave up his roots in his religious faith and held on to them valiantly in his life-long pilgrimage toward the realization of Truth. He focused his attention on the necessity of living religiously. His religious consciousness was both mystical and prophetic; he made social life his field of research. He insisted on truth and nonviolence in every sphere of life. For him, religion and truth were so coequal that his religion may be said to be the religion of truth; and the way to it was *ahiṁsā*, nonviolence. Thus, truth and nonviolence constituted "the essence of his faith — twin suns around which all the lesser planets of his faith revolved."[1] It is therefore not by accident that Gandhi called his autobiography *The Story of My Experiments with Truth.*

The environment into which the child Mohandas Gandhi was born had certain elements that moulded and shaped his life and mind. He belonged to a highly respected vaiśya family; he was a Vaiṣṇava by faith. The members of his family were noted more for piety and honest living than for wealth or scholarship. Kaba Gandhi, the father of Mohandas, had no education save that of experience;[2] he was truthful, brave, and generous, but short-tempered.[3] He rose to be Dewan of Rajkot and later of Vankaner in Kathiawar.

Mohandas' mother was a deeply religious woman who went to the temple daily, never took a meal before prayer, and frequently undertook fasts, which she kept faithfully. Gandhi had a deep and steadfast love for his mother. The gentleness of her character and her deep piety made a profound impression on him from his earliest years. Throughout his life, he was concerned with the cultivation and appreciation of at least three virtues of the Hindu faith in which he was brought up by his mother: *ahiṁsā* (nonviolence), *brahmacharya* (celibacy), and *aparigraha* (non-acquisition). It was in such a background that his early years were spent. The roots of his emotional makeup and intellectual creativity lay in Hindu religious texts like the Rāmāyaṇa and Mahābhārata, the Bhagavadgītā, the Upaniṣads, and the *Vaiṣṇava* lyrics. C. F. Andrews observes, "The more we study Mahatma Gandhi's own life and teaching, the more certain it becomes that the Hindu religion has been the greatest of all influences in shaping his idea and actions. He is in no sense a literalist or a fundamentalist in his adherence to the Hindu scriptures. His extraordinary tolerance and sympathy with other faiths colours his whole outlook on human life, and makes him at times seem nearer to the acceptance of an indeterminate position than he really is. But his mother's influence as a devout and gentle Hindu saint perpetually returns to his mind and conscience, making the fragrance of the ancient Hindu texts so sweet that nothing else in the world can compare with them, to his own imagination, in beauty and truth and sweetness."[4]

At school, he was shy and kept himself aloof from his classmates. He liked to go to plays. The play *Harischandra*, based on a story from the epic Mahābhārata, had aroused his imagination in his early years. The ordeals undergone by Harischandra for his devotion to truth made a deep impression on him. He asked himself, "Why should not all be truthful like Harischandra?"[5]

In the life of the Gandhi family, religion played a vital part. In Kathiawar, Jainism exercised an enduring influence along with Vaiṣṇavism. Gandhi's nonviolence, vegetarianism, and many other traits of his religious personality date from his very early years. His father had friends in all faiths, who visited him frequently for religious discussions. Young Mohandas, while attending on his father, listened to these discussions with Hindus, Muslims, Parsis, Jains, and adherents of other religions. During this period, he also read the *Rāmāyaṇa*, the *Bhāgavata*, and the *Manusmṛti* from his father's library. All these made him very tolerant in his religious ideas, and unsectarian in nature. He later wrote, "In Rajkot, however, I got an early grounding in toleration for all branches of Hinduism and sister religions. For my father and mother would visit the *Haveli* as also Shiva's and Rāma's temples, and would take or send us youngsters there. Jain monks also would pay frequent visits to my father, and would go even out of their way to accept food from us — non-Jains."[6] But his earliest impressions of Christianity were disturbing. "In those days, Christian missionaries used to stand in a corner near the high school and hold forth, pouring abuse on Hindus and their Gods,"[7] and many Hindus converted to Christianity ate beef and drank liquor.

His old nurse, Rambha, advised him to take refuge in *Rāmanāma* (repetition of the name of Rāma), to be rid of his childhood fears that assailed him at night. In his later days, he found the repetition of *Rāmanāma* a source of great strength and solace and it became a part of his daily life. Indeed it was Rāma that he called upon when his soul took flight to God.

In his teens, Gandhi was for some time drawn towards atheism. His doubts were not adequately answered by the religious writings that came his way. He found, for instance, that Manu approved of meat-eating. But even then, he had a regard for morality as the basis of all things, and for truth as the substance of morality. "Truth became my sole objective," he wrote. "It began to grow in magnitude every day, and my definition of it also has been ever widening."[8]

Before he left for England in 1888, to qualify himself as a barrister, his mother made him take three solemn oaths; "not to touch wine, woman, and meat."[9] This vow he kept religiously despite many temptations to break it.

Because of his journey to a foreign land, his own caste people excommunicated him. And even though, later, he performed purificatory rites, orthodox prejudice kept him out of the caste fold. This caste denial caused no resentment in him. It rather taught him how artificial the barriers of caste were, and he came to realize intensely the cruelty of seeking to restrict human fellowship.

In studying the early years of Gandhi's life, one can easily see in them the seeds that later flowered into full bloom. "His innate love of truth, desire for the freedom of his Motherland, love of simple things and simple people, passion for purity, even to austerity, tried courage and quiet moral strength — all these qualities were struggling within him to find suitable expression in a field of labour big enough to call them to play."[10]

In England, he spent a large part of his time cultivating the personal acquaintance of several men who had made their mark in the fields of religion and ethics — Theosophists, Christians, even atheists. He joined the Vegetarian Society of England and started a Vegetarian Club in his locality (Bayswater) and became its secretary, and was an ardent propagandist for vegetarianism. The literature of the Theosophists introduced him to the religious movement for the unity of religions. Edwin Arnold's *The Light of Asia*, about the life of the Buddha, made a lasting impression on him, and his English version of the Bhagavadgītā, *The Song Celestial*, stirred him so deeply that for the rest of his life it became his constant guide. He was also much moved by the teachings of the New Testament and especially the Sermon on the Mount. The verses, "But I say unto you, that ye resist not evil; but whosoever shall smite thee on thy right cheek, turn to him the other also," went straight to his heart. Gandhi wrote later about this experience, "My young mind tried to unify the teaching of the Gītā, *The Light of Asia*, and the Sermon on the Mount. That renunciation was the highest form of religion appealed to me greatly."[11] Further, from Carlyle's *Heroes and Hero Worship* he learned of Muhammad's "greatness, bravery and austere living."[12] He also read Washington Irving's *Life of Mahomet and His Successors*. These books raised Muhammad in his estimation. He also gained more and more knowledge of different religious traditions. From them, he received some of the basic principles of his life, and he became inclined towards a life in which East and West could meet.

Gandhi's life in South Africa presented to him direct experience of the bad as well as the good aspects of religion. He had hardly set foot in South Africa, in the spring of 1891, when he became involved in the racial and color conflict. One experience in South Africa changed the course of his life. He was traveling in a train with a first-class ticket, and he was turned out of his compartment to make way for a white passenger. In the midnight cold of Maritzburg, he was not allowed even to enter a waiting room, because of the color of his skin. Then the moment of decision came: should he go back to India or stay in South Africa and start a life-long struggle for human justice? He decided to stay and fight injustice, and not to flee. Once, when he was kicked by a policeman off a footpath near President Kruger's house without the slightest warning, he said to himself, "The hardship to which I am subjected is superficial — only a symptom of the deep disease of color prejudice. I should try, if possible, to root out the disease and suffer hardships in the process."[13]

In South Africa, Gandhi met adherents of a variety of Christian sects; a Quaker who wanted to rescue him from ignorance, a Plymouth Brother, for whom religion was not necessarily related to morality, and so forth. But Gandhi was looking for the spirit of the Sermon on the Mount in modern Christianity.

He developed a passion for serving the poor. He wrote, "If I found myself entirely absorbed in the service of the community, the reason behind it was my desire for self-realization. I had made the religion of service my own as I felt that God could be realized only through service. ... I had gone to South Africa for travel, for finding an escape from Kathiawad intrigues and for gaining my livelihood. But, as I have said, I found myself in search of God and striving for self-realization.[14] I began to realize more and more the infinite possibilities of universal love."[15]

When the Boer War began in 1899, Gandhi organized an Indian Ambulance Corps and offered its services to the authorities. In 1904, when plague broke out in Johannesburg, he closed his law office and devoted himself to sanitary work and the evacuation and nursing of the victims. In 1906, when the Zulu rebellion occurred in Natal, he organized from among the Indian community a stretcher-bearer company and offered its services to the Government, which accepted it with Gandhi as the Sergeant Major.

At Johannesburg Gandhi had a flourishing law practice. He gained increasing influence. His words were heeded by a large portion of Indians in South Africa. One would perhaps expect such a person to be satisfied with such achievements, but Gandhi was not. There was a deep hunger in him that could not be satisfied by worldly success. He could find no abiding satisfaction in material gain.

John Ruskin's *Unto This Last* (which Gandhi summarized later in Gujarati under the title *Sarvodaya*) makes a critical study of modern civilization and pleads passionately for new social values. It made a decisive impression on him. A Mr. Polak had lent him a copy of the book to read during one of his journeys from Johannesburg to Durban. "The book was impossible to lay aside; once I had begun it, it gripped me. I could not get any sleep that night. I determined to change my life in accordance with the ideals of that book. ... I believe that I discovered some of my deepest convictions reflected in this great book of Ruskin, and that is why it so captured me and made me transform my life."[16] He realized "that a life of labour, i.e., the life of the tiller of the soil and the handicraftsman is the life worth living."[17] It was an important event in Gandhi's life. He got up at dawn that morning and resolved to give up his career as a successful lawyer in order to become an Indian peasant; he decided to transform his whole mode of existence, his profession, and even his private life.

To realize the new way of life, he established an āshram, the Phoenix Settlement, near Durban. It was a little colony consisting of Indian and European friends and colleagues who lived and worked happily together in public service. While carrying on his public work, he was slowly revolutionizing his private life. A passion for simplicity and service took hold of him. He cut down the expenditure of his household, became his own barber and washerman, and taught his children at home without sending them to any school. He volunteered to become a compounder and a nurse in a charitable hospital and gave two hours of his time in the morning to this work. It was at this time that Gandhi took his vow for *brahmacharya* (celibacy) for life, to be able to devote himself solely to the love and service of his fellow men.

Possibly, one of the persons who exercised a most decisive influence during this period was Tolstoy. Gandhi read *The Kingdom of God Is Within You* during his first year in Africa while he lived in Pretoria. The teaching of the book that the Sermon on the Mount was a sufficient guide to life, along with its profound sorrow concerning war, conscription, injustice, and oppression — was as if written for Gandhi. In Durban, he read some other later works of Tolstoy. *The Gospels in Brief* and *What to Do* made a deep impression on him. In answering an American correspondent, he later refers to this and some other influences, "You have given me a teacher in Thoreau, who furnished me through his essay on the 'Duty of Civil-disobedience' scientific confirmation of what I was doing in South Africa. Great Britain gave me Ruskin, whose *Unto This Last* transformed me overnight from a lawyer and city dweller into a rustic living away from Durban on a farm, three miles from the nearest railway station; and Russia gave me in Tolstoy a teacher who furnished a reasoned basis for my nonviolence. Tolstoy blessed my movement in South Africa when it was still in its infancy and of whose wonderful possibilities I had yet to learn. It was he who has prophesied in his letter to me that I was leading a movement which was destined to bring a message of hope to the downtrodden people of the earth."[18]

Gandhi shaped a new political tool for the masses, *satyāgraha*. The South African Indians under the leadership of Gandhi launched a nonviolent struggle against the discrimination to which the Transvaal Government was subjecting them. Gandhi was arrested on the orders of General Smuts. This was his first experience of prison life (1908). After a protracted struggle for the rights of the Indians in South Africa, he achieved his first great victory. It is during this eventful period of his life that the basic outline of his religious and moral philosophy was drawn in the light of his spiritual and practical experience.

On returning to India, he founded another āshram at Sabarmati, Satyāgraha Āshram, with some of his fellow workers from Phoenix. All the members of the āshram were pledged to nonviolence, vegetarianism, non-possession, etc. He conducted experiments, on a vast scale, for the realization of truth through love and service of men. He started, one after another, a number of movements : hand-spinning, basic education, a campaign for Hindustani as the national language of India, a movement for the uplift of untouchables, and one for the training of women in village service. Gandhi invited an untouchable family to the āshram and its members were accepted as equals by the colony. This admission of untouchables to the āshram caused a good deal of opposition in the country against Gandhi. But in all these things he was undaunted, because he was prompted by religious longing. He wrote, "What I want to achieve—what I have been striving and pining to achieve these thirty years — is self-realization, to see God face to face, to attain *Moksha*. I live and move and have my being in pursuit of this goal. All that I do by way of speaking and writing, and all my ventures in the political field are directed to this same end."[19]

Even while Gandhi was engaged in struggles that were not apparently religious in character (like the "Salt Satyāgraha" or the "Quit India Programme"), his dominant motive was a religious one; of doing everything in a spirit of dedication to God. He wrote, "Man's ultimate aim is the realization of God, and all his activities, social, religious, have to be guided by the ultimate aim of the vision of God. The immediate service of all human beings becomes a necessary part of the endeavor, simply because the only way to find God is to see Him in His creation and be one with it. This can only be done by service of all. I am part and parcel of the whole and I cannot find Him apart from the rest of humanity. My countrymen are my nearest neighbors. They have become so helpless, so resourceless, so inert that I must concentrate myself on serving them. If I could persuade myself that I could find Him in a Himalayan cave I would proceed there immediately, but I know that I cannot find Him apart from humanity."[20]

Gandhi, all through his life, devoted much time and energy to the promotion of Hindu-Muslim unity. He once fasted for three weeks for this cause. He said, "My penance is the prayer of a bleeding heart... it is a warning to Hindus and Muslims who have professed to love me." He wrote, "If not during my lifetime, I know after my death both Hindus and Muslims will bear witness that I had never ceased to yearn after communal peace."[21] Earlier, he had supported the Muslims in the Khilafat Movement and agitated for the release of the Ali brothers. C. F. Andrews observes, "During one period of the Non-Cooperation Movement, he made the nearest approach to Islam that has ever been made by Hinduism in recent times. He found that the devout followers of Islam, who revered the Caliph at Constantinople as the Head of their religion, had been outraged by the ignominious terms of surrender imposed upon the Command of the Faithful at the end of the war; for the victorious destroyed much of the Caliph's temporal authority, thus threatening it at its very center." He adds, "At this point, Mahatma Gandhi, whose one intense longing had always been to unite Hindus and Mussalmans together, in one common Indian nation, seized the psychological opportunity of supporting the Mussalmans in what he held to be a righteous cause. He promised them his entire devotion on behalf of their Caliph and gave himself whole-heartedly to them. Thus, this Khilafat question, which was agitating Islam, in India became for a time the direct means of a cordial reconciliation."[22]

Thanks to Gandhi's efforts, India achieved political freedom in August 1947 through nonviolent means. India became a friend on equal terms with England. Thanks also to the statesmanship of the British Labour Party, a great imperial power surrendered its domain smoothly and peacefully to the people it had governed for nearly two centuries. But Gandhi was then not in Delhi to celebrate the coming of Independence. He was in Noakhali in Bengal giving strength and hope to those who were sorrow-laden, endeavoring to eliminate the distress of those who were victims of religious hatred.

In the wake of the partition of the country, hundreds of thousands of Hindus and Muslims were killed in the Punjab, Bengal, and Bihar. Gandhi threw himself into the struggle to heal the breach between the two communities. He toured in the riot-affected areas preaching the need for peace and good will. The mob attacked Gandhi himself in Calcutta. He had become the symbol of the Hindu intransigence to angry Muslims, while his efforts to protect Muslims infuriated the suffering Hindus. He began a fast in Calcutta and worked a miracle. Lord Mountbatten, then the Governor-General of India, wrote to Gandhi, "In the Punjab, we have 55,000 soldiers and large-scale rioting on our hands. In Bengal our forces consist of one man, and there is no rioting."[23]

Then he traveled to Delhi; the capital was ringed with violence and shaken by murders. He spoke to the crowds; he explained that a Hindu, a Muslim, and a Christian were all brothers, sons of the same God. And he started another fast the eighteenth and the last of his life. He had reached the age of 78. He broke the fast only when he received definite assurances from Hindu and Muslim leaders that they would do their utmost to stop violence, and when India paid over Pakistan's share in the assets of the undivided State (about 40 million pounds).

On Friday, January 30, 1948, at five o'clock in the evening, when he went out for his daily prayer meeting, a Hindu moved towards Gandhi and fired three shots with a revolver. The first shot hit Gandhi in his abdomen. He muttered "Hē Rām, Hē Rām"; blood gushed from his abdomen and then from his heart. As he was brought into the house he lost consciousness.

It was a Hindu that had killed the Mahatma, a radical Hindu who could not bear Gandhi's insistence that violence and force should not be used against Muslims living in India. A saint had been killed by his own people.

Gandhi was not unaware of the magnitude of the problem with which he was dealing. He had to face religious fanaticism and bigotry, superstition and ignorance, selfishness and hypocrisy, even atheism and indifferentism. Many a time his was a voice crying in the wilderness. His plea for tolerance (nonviolence) and reverence towards the faith of other men often fell on deaf ears. It is difficult to say how far Gandhi succeeded in establishing the relationship of love and reverence between Hindus and Muslims in India. Obviously, much more remains to be done. As he often used to say, he was only beginning the experiment with nonviolence. He was just trying to put people on the road.

Gandhi wanted harmony and peace to be established not merely between Hindus and Muslims, but among the adherents of all the great religions of the world. He once wrote, "Hindu-Muslim unity means not only unity between Hindus and Mussalmans, but between all those who believe India to be their home — no matter to what faith they belong."[24] In fact, the problem that faced Gandhi in India is a world problem. With the annihilation of distance by modern science and technology, the world has become a single unit. The meeting of religions, therefore, is not confined to India only; it is now a universal encounter. The problem of the mutual relationships of the religions can no more be postponed or sidestepped. In the interests of lasting peace and harmony among the peoples of the world, the problem has to be successfully tackled. This demands a sympathetic study and understanding, on the part of believers of all faiths, of the different religions of the world. In this connection, Gandhi's life and example throw some fresh light on the problem and bring a new and sensitive approach to its solution based on mutual understanding. An attempt will be made in the following pages to spell out and critically examine Gandhi's approach to comparative religion and inter-religious relations.

**References**

1. Horace Alexander in his introduction to *Mahatma Gandhi's Ideas* by C. F. Andrews, Allen and Unwin, London, 1949, p. 4.
2. M. K. Gandhi, *An Autobiography*, Beacon Press, Boston, 1966, p. 4.
3. *Ibid.*, p. 3.
4. C. F. Andrews, *op. cit.*, p. 60.
5. M. K. Gandhi, *op. cit.*, p. 7.
6. *Ibid.*, p. 33.
7. *Ibid.*, p. 33.
8. *Ibid.*, p. 34.
9. *Ibid.*, p. 39.
10. Rushbrook Williams, *Great Men of India*, The Home Library Club, Bombay, p. 316.
11. M. K. Gandhi, *op. cit.*, p. 69.
12. *Ibid.*, p. 69.
13. *Ibid.*, p. 163.
14. *Ibid.*, p. 158.
15. *Ibid.*, p. 160.
16. *Ibid.*, p. 288-289.
17. *Ibid.*, p. 299.
18. D. G. Tendulkar, *Mahatma Gandhi*, Vitthalbhai K. Jhaveri & Tendulkar, Bombay, 1953, Vol. 6, p. 177.
19. M. K. Gandhi, *op. cit.*, p. xii.
20. *Harijan*, 29-8-1936.
21. *Ibid.*, 12-10-1935.
22. C. F. Andrews, *op. cit.*, pp. 55-57.
23. Pyarelal, *Mahatma Gandhi — The Last Phase*, Navajivan Publishing House, Ahmedabad, 1958, Vol. II, p. 382.
24. *Young India*, 16-4-1931.

## Chapter 2

# GANDHI'S COMPARATIVE STUDY OF RELIGIONS

### (i) HINDUISM

GANDHI claimed that he was not only a Hindu, but also a Muslim, a Christian, and a Buddhist. Such a position would be considered absurd in the Semitic traditions. But Gandhi was not claiming to be a Mussalman or a Christian in the accept ed sense of the term. His claim was simply that, though a Hindu by birth and conviction, he could appreciate and assimilate all that in Islam and Christianity and Buddhism and other religions he found to be precious. He welcomed the best in every tradition. He thought that the discovery of the merits and points of agreements in other religions would contribute greatly to the enriching of each religion and to the development of the true religious attitude in the votaries of all religions. He specially pointed to the need for inner purification in every religion. Thus inevitably he became a reformer of his own religious tradition.

By study and observation, Gandhi came to know only too well the corruption and degradation that had crept into Hinduism in practice. He knew the elements in it that had become obsolete and had lost their value in the context of modern times. But the Hinduism that was dear to him was a purified Hinduism, purified and sanctified in the crucible of his life and thought. He wrote, "What we see today is not pure Hinduism, but often a parody of it."[1] All the same, he was aware of its perpetual and basic vitality, which had successfully survived the vicissitudes of history for over five thousand years. He could find in it elements of the highest quality. "There is something in Hinduism that has kept it alive up till now. It has witnessed the fall of the Babylonian, Syrian, Persian, and Egyptian civilizations. Cast a look around you. Where is Rome or Greece? Can you find today anywhere the Italy of Gibbon, or the ancient

Rome, for Rome was Italy ? Then come to India; let one go through the most ancient records and then look around you and he would be constrained to say, 'Yes, I see ancient India still living.' True, there are dung-heaps too, here and there; but there are rich treasures buried beneath them. And the reason why it has survived is that the end which Hinduism set before it was development not along material lines but spiritual lines."[2]

Hinduism is like a federation of different religious creeds, theological schools, and sectarian faiths that have survived in India from ancient times. It represents almost every stage in the evolution of humanity's search for God. Even animistic cults flourish alongside of the highest monotheistic as well as monistic religion. Every form of worship is considered by the Hindus a useful stepping stone to a higher form, and hence each form is tolerated with a kindly eye and a deep understanding, as suitable at some stage of spiritual growth. Hinduism does not insist on uniformity of thought or practice. It recognizes the need for different planes of religious expression in a world where men are in different stages of spiritual development. In Gandhi's view, "Hinduism is a grand evolutionary process and not a narrow creed." Further , "Hinduism is a living organism liable to growth and decay, and subject to the laws of Nature. One and indivisible at the root, it has grown into a vast tree with innumerable branches. The changes in the season affect it. It has its autumn and summer, its winter and spring."[3] In the words of Max Müller, "This religion has room for almost every religion, nay it embraces them all." In its all-embracing fold, it contains all stages of social and religious evolution. It has stood for a principle of comprehension and synthesis by which differences are reconciled as parts of a common complex.

Hinduism does not pin its faith on a single book or on a single prophet. It has no particular founder or scripture, for the approach towards Truth is broad-based on an ever-expanding vision and experience of the Divine. The Divine has existed without beginning or end. The Omnipotent Spirit asserts itself in various forms. Hinduism considers all religions as true and necessary insofar as they help the spiritual development of humanity in different times and climes. It embraces in its compass all the various means by which man can approach God.

It insists on the truth acknowledged by all the religions, viz., that He is in all men and in all things and in Him all live and move and have their being. Further, each person is exhorted to pursue salvation by the light of his own religious faith and experience. It has no official creed connected with any one particular teacher. According to Gandhi, "Hinduism is not a codified religion. We have in Hinduism hundreds and thousands of books whose names even we do not know, which go under the name of *Śāstras*."[4] In the words of Dr. Sarvepalli Radhakrishnan, "Hinduism is more a way of life than a form of thought. While it gives absolute liberty in the world of thought, it enjoins a strict code of practice."[5] He adds, "It insists not on religious conformity but on a spiritual and ethical outlook on life."[6]

No doubt, Hinduism comprises many creeds and ideologies. But they are considered as different interpretations of the one Reality and different ways to reach the same goal. The various features displayed by these creeds are seen as suited to local needs and relative to circumstances of time and place. In fact, this very heterogeneity of content in Hinduism makes for tolerance. As Dr. Radhakrishnan says, "Hinduism has come to be a tapestry of the most variegated tissues and almost endless diversity of hues."[7] And so, "On the principle that the very best is not the enemy of the good, Hinduism accepts all forms of belief and lifts them up to a higher level."[8] In the words of Gandhi, "Hinduism is not an exclusive religion. In it there is room for the worship of all prophets of the world. It is not a missionary religion in the ordinary sense of the term. It has no doubt many tribes in its fold, but this absorption has been of an evolutionary, imperceptible character. Hinduism tells everyone to worship God according to his faith or *dharma*, and so lives at peace with all religions."[9]

Hinduism as Gandhi conceived it is something more than the Hinduism of history. Gandhi often used the same word with a new connotation. He gave to Hinduism a new dimension of the spirit by continually relating it to evolving and advancing truth. He accepted whatever was beautiful and good and true wherever found. Everything that harmonized with truth and the eternal moral laws was acceptable to him. He himself claimed to be an orthodox Hindu on his own terms, though the so-called orthodox Hindus disputed his claim. Obviously, his *sanātana* (orthodox) Hinduism was of a different type from the conventional; else he could not have become the revolutionary champion of the depressed and oppressed castes in India that he was. Still less could he have developed his spiritual kinship with the Buddha, Christ, and Muhammad. Jawaharlal Nehru observes, "Gandhi was essentially a man of religion, a Hindu to the innermost depths of his being, and yet his conception of religion had nothing to do with any dogma or custom or ritual."[10] Gandhi's view of Hinduism was much deeper and broader than Hinduism as generally understood. He made it quite clear in what sense he was an orthodox Hindu. "If orthodox Hinduism can mean an incessant striving to live Hinduism to the best of one's lights, then I do claim to be an orthodox Hindu. I am also an orthodox Hindu in the sense in which the author of the Mahābhārata, the great Vyāsa would have it. He has said somewhere in the Mahābhārata to this effect: put truth in one scale and all sacrifices whatever in the other; that scale which contains truth will outweigh the one that contains all the sacrifices put together, not excluding *Rājasūya* and *Aśvamedha Yajña.* And if the Mahābhārata may be accepted as the fifth Veda, then I claim to be an orthodox Hindu because every moment of the twenty-four hours of my life, I am endeavoring to follow truth, counting no cost too great."[11] Elsewhere he claims, "I call myself a *sanātani* Hindu because, (1) I believe in the Vedas, the Upaniṣads, the Purāṇas and all that goes by the name of Hindu scriptures, and therefore in Avatāras and rebirth; (2) I believe in the *varṇāśrama dharma* in a sense, in my opinion, strictly Vedic but not in its present popular and crude sense; (3) I believe in the protection of the cow in its much larger sense than the popular; (4) I do not disbelieve in idol worship."[12]

Hindus hold that personal descriptions of God are qualities people admire in human beings, and since they believe that God is infinitely good, they surmise that God has an unlimited amount of admirable qualities. Many persons use the term "God" to mean a personalized God, i.e., one who has the characteristics of a human person. For example, we are familiar with expressions like "God loves," "God is merciful", "the hand of God," etc. There are in Hinduism personal gods to be worshiped by those who so desire. But the Hindu also holds that if we use the term God to mean the Reality, it is beyond all such human characterizations. The personal gods are all subordinate to the *Paramātman* or Oversoul or Brahman. And even while they worship the personal gods, the Hindus never fail to realize that they are only fractions of the one and the only *Parabrahman.* The real function of the worship of a personal God and images is to direct the worshiper ultimately to the knowledge of God Himself. Gandhi observes, "I have said that I do not disbelieve in idol worship. An idol does not excite any feeling of veneration in me. But I think that idol worship is a part of human nature. We hanker after symbolism. Why should one be more composed in a Church than elsewhere ? Images are an aid to worship. No Hindu considers an image to be God. I do not consider idol worship is sin."[13]

Gandhi believed that the first verse of the *Īśopaniṣad* contains the whole essence of Hinduism. The verse reads:

> *Īśāvāsyamidam sarvam yatkincha jagatyām jagat,*
> *Tena tyaktena bhuñjīthā mā gṛdhaḥ kasya svit dhanam.*
>
> (Whatever exists in this changing universe, all that is embraced by the Lord; enjoy by renouncing it; covet not anybody's wealth.)

According to Gandhi, "The *mantra* describes God as the Creator, the Ruler and the Lord. The seer to whom this *mantra* or verse was revealed was not satisfied with the magnificent statement that God was to be found everywhere. But he went further and said: 'Since God pervades everything nothing belongs to you, not even your own body. God is the undisputed, unchallengeable Master of everything you possess.' And so when a person who calls himself a Hindu goes through the process of regeneration or a second birth, as Christians would call it, he has to perform a dedication or renunciation of all that he has in ignorance called his own property. And then when he has performed this act of dedication or renunciation, he is told he will win a reward in the shape of God taking good care of what he will require for food, clothing, or housing. Therefore the condition of enjoyment or use of the necessities of life is their dedication or renunciation and that dedication or renunciation has got to be done from day to day, lest we may in this busy world forget the central fact of life. And to crown all, the seer says: 'Covet not anybody's riches.' I suggest to you that the truth that is embedded in this very short *mantra* is calculated to satisfy the highest cravings of every human being whether they have reference to this world or to the next. I have in my search of the scriptures of the world found nothing to add to this *mantra*. Looking back upon all the little I have read of the scriptures — it is precious little, I confess — I feel that everything good in all the scriptures is derived from this *mantra*. If it is universal brotherhood — not only brotherhood of all human beings, but of all living beings — I find it in this *mantra*. If it is unshakable faith in the Lord and Master — and all the adjectives you think of — I find it in this *mantra*. If it is the idea of complete surrender to God and of the faith that He will supply all that I need, then again I say, I find it in this *mantra*. Since He pervades every fiber of my being and of all of you, I derive from it the doctrine of equality of all creatures on earth and it should satisfy the cravings of all philosophical communists. This *mantra* tells me that I cannot hold as mine anything that belongs to God, and if my life and that of all who believe in this *mantra* has to be a life of perfect dedication, it follows that it will have to be a life of continual service of our fellow-creatures." He adds, "This I say is my faith and should be the faith of all who call themselves Hindus."[14]

Answering a question from an American correspondent, as to the reasons for his choice to remain a Hindu, Gandhi observes, "Believing as I do in the influence of heredity, being born in a Hindu family, I have remained a Hindu. I should reject it, if I found it inconsistent with my moral sense or my spiritual growth. On examination I have found it to be the most tolerant of all religions known to me. Its freedom from dogma makes a forcible appeal to me inasmuch as it gives the votary the largest scope for self-expression. Not being an exclusive religion it enables followers of that faith not merely to respect all other religions, but it also enables them to admire and assimilate whatever may be good in other faiths. Nonviolence is common to all the religions, but it has found the highest expression and application in Hinduism (I do not regard Jainism or

Buddhism as separate from Hinduism). Hinduism believes in the oneness not merely of all human life, but in the oneness of all that lives. Its worship of cow is, in my opinion, its unique contribution to the evolution of humanitarianism. It is a practical application of the belief in the oneness and, therefore, sacredness of all life. The great belief in transmigration is a direct consequence of that belief."[15]

Gandhi's conception of Hinduism had no place for untouchability. He saw in the prevalent plight of the untouchables nothing but a travesty of religion and a blot on Hinduism. "I have never been able to reconcile myself to untouchability. I have always regarded it as an excrescence."[16] He staked his all for the uplift of the depressed and the suppressed castes in India. Within a lifetime, Gandhi by his teachings, personal example, and reforming zeal transformed the untouchables into a fearless, progressive, and vital element of the Indian nation. And insofar as this transformation was in relation to the so-called lowest in the Hindu community, its effect touched every stratum of Indian society, thus setting in motion one of the most powerful liberalizing forces in religion in the whole world. He declared, "Untouchability is repugnant to reason and to the instinct of mercy, pity, and love. A religion that establishes the worship of the cow cannot possibly countenance or warrant a cruel and inhuman boycott of human beings. And I should be content to be torn to pieces rather than to disown the suppressed classes. Hindus will certainly never deserve freedom, nor get it, if they allow this noble religion to be disgraced by the retention of the taint of untouchability. And as I love Hinduism dearer than life itself, the taint has become for me an intolerable burden. Let us not deny God by denying a fifth of our race the right of association on equal footing."[17]

Hinduism stresses the unity of existence. It points to a way of life where the individual may be enabled to exist in tune with the infinite. The ground of all existence is Brahman. Hinduism teaches that each person is important to all other persons and living beings. This means that each must learn to rise above his own selfish interests and do his duty to others whatever the cost. The enlightened person finds release by meditating on Brahman and by conquering the little self and its vanities by purity of life. Love of all living beings leads to love of God. According to the Gītā, "When one sees Me everywhere and everything in Me, I am never lost to him and he is never lost to Me."[18] This insistence on oneness, in Hinduism, has been one of its unique features. "The chief value of Hinduism lies in holding the actual belief that all life (not only human beings but all sentient beings) is one, i.e., all life coming from one universal source, call it Allah, God, or *Parameśvara.* ... This unity of life is a peculiarity of Hinduism which confines salvation not to human beings alone, but says that it is possible for all God's creatures. It may be that it is not possible, save through the human form, but that does not make man the Lord of creation. It makes him the servant of God's creation. Now when we talk of brotherhood of man, we stop there and feel that all other life is there for man to exploit for his own purposes. But Hinduism excludes all exploitation. There is no limit whatsoever to the measure of sacrifice that one may make in order to realize this oneness with all life, but certainly the immensity of the ideal sets a limit to your wants."[19] Hinduism holds that a life of wealth and luxury does not often bring out the best in man. In the midst of great prosperity there suddenly comes to the Hindu a call for renunciation. This renunciation is specially noble when it means renunciation for the sake of service of humanity. Such indeed was Gandhi's own life in its simplicity, devotion to truth, and nonviolence evoking the homage of people all over the world.

All the great religions teach love of man; but Hinduism teaches love of animals as well. That is why many devout Hindus never eat meat. They feel killing an animal is wrong. The animal has as much right to live as man. According to Gandhi, "cow protection" is the gift of Hinduism to the world. It is a distinctive contribution to the world's religious ideas. "Cow" to him meant the entire subhuman world. It meant "the protection of the weak and the helpless."[20] To Gandhi, "cow protection" had a very wide significance. "I am not ready to believe that by merely protecting the animal cow, one can attain *Mokṣa,* for *Mokṣa* one must completely get rid of one's lower feelings like attachment, hatred, anger, jealousy, etc. It follows, therefore, that the meaning of cow protection in terms of *Mokṣa* must be much wider and far more comprehensive than is commonly supposed. The cow protection which can bring one *Mokṣa* must, from its very nature, include the protection of everything that feels. Therefore in my opinion every little breach of the *ahiṁsā* principle, like causing hurt by harsh speech to anyone, man, woman or child, to cause pain to the weakest and the most insignificant creature on earth, would be a breach of the principle of cow protection, would be tantamount to the sin of beef eating, differing from it in degree, if at all, rather than in kind. That being so, I hold that with all our passions let loose we cannot today claim to be following the principle of cow protection."[21]

Gandhi was in favour of *varṇāśrama* in its original sense. Originally the word indicated only a division of labor in society and a sort of economic arrangement. The four social groups were instituted by the *Smṛtis*: the priestly class devoted to studies and religious pursuits leading pure and simple lives, the ruling and the soldier class, the commercial and wealth-producing class, and the serving class (*Brāhmaṇa*, *Kshatriya*, *Vaiśya*, and *Śūdra*). These social groups were of a flexible nature and in consonance with the aptitudes and abilities of people. But later the whole system fell into abuse and became divided into watertight compartments, confining the free life of men in a static state. During the age of the *dharmasāśtras* and later there developed a number of *jātis*, sub-castes, within the four castes, and today we find hundreds of castes and sub-castes in Hindu society. In actual life, these rigid divisions of caste often lead to cruel injustice and discrimination.

Gandhi was the foremost to realize the terrible abuses that had crept into the *varṇāśrama dharma* and to offer relentless battle against them. In his very insistence on truth and non-violence, he focused a revealing light on the cruelties of the present caste system. The caste system was, he thought, opposed to the basic concept of love. Therefore he emphasized that Hindus must break loose from the shackles of the past, retain all that is good, and mercilessly disregard the rest. He often declared that unless Hinduism washed away the dirt of the distinction between the high and low it cannot survive. It is necessary here to remember the distinction between *Varṇāśrama dharma* and the caste system. Gandhi considered the latter as a caricature of the former.

Gandhi also reminded the Hindus of their responsibility in the context of the variety and the multiplicity of religious traditions that have always existed in India. He emphasized the underlying unity of all religions and the importance of a spiritual search to find the eternal behind the trivial and the temporary. He exhorted the Hindus: "You have to live in a world which has Christians and Mussalmans, great communities owning great faiths. You have to live in the midst of these whether they are two per cent or twenty per cent. And if I know Hinduism aright, Hinduism is nothing if it is not tolerant and generous to every other faith. And seeing that you are in a vast majority, it is up to you to make advances and settle all your disputes. And if you will get rid of the wretched caste spirit which has crept into Hinduism you will find that all the difficulties will disappear."[22]

## (ii) BUDDHISM

When human nature revolts against the oppressive rules and formalities of religion, when mere external observances no longer satisfy, then there arises a need for reformation of a tradition, and a great teacher often appears on the human scene to stimulate and uplift mankind. One such was the Buddha. The Buddha did not claim to be the originator of a new religion. What he did was to reform and even revolutionize Hinduism as prevalent in his day. His own life and his ethical fervor were directed to uplifting "the poorest, the lowliest, and the lost." He proved to be a great fructifying force in religious life. He never rejected Hinduism, but "gave it a new life and a new interpretation."[1] As a matter of fact, he was born a Hindu and was brought up in the Hindu atmosphere and had followed Hindu precepts and teachings; he was saturated in the basic concepts and practices of Hinduism. The twin doctrines of *karma* and *saṁsāra*, involving transmigration of souls according to one's deeds, became the twin foundations of the new religion as they were of the old. Therefore Buddhism could never be completely independent of Hinduism.

The religious language of the Buddhist scriptures is just as characteristically Hindu as the Christian scriptures are Jewish. Much of the Buddhist thought is identical with much Hindu thought. The Buddha led a protestant movement in Hinduism. He was dissatisfied with certain elements in Hinduism such as extreme ritualism, animal sacrifices, and severe ascetic practices; these, he felt, were useless and turned away from them. True religion and morality were lost in a heap of meaningless rites, childish superstitions, and futile discussions. The Buddha could not believe that one's sins could be forgiven by shedding the blood of innocent animals or that one's sins could be expiated by the prayers of another man who is paid to pray. Gandhi wrote, "The one thing that the Buddha showed India was that God was not a God who can be appeased by the sacrifice of innocent animals. On the contrary, he held that those who sacrificed animals in the hope of pleasing God were guilty of a double sin."[2]

The Buddha was of the view that no external factor could bring about the enlightenment of the soul. He revolted against the formalism and ritualism of Brâhmanism in India. He saw that the brâhmins had become preoccupied more with outward forms than with the search for truth. Gandhi observed, "He [the Buddha] was saturated with the best that was in Hinduism, and he gave life to some of the teachings that were buried in the Vedas and were overgrown with weeds. His great Hindu spirit cut its way through the forest of words, meaningless words, which had overlaid the golden truth that was in the Vedas. He made some of the words in the Vedas yield a meaning to which the men of his generation were utter strangers, and he found in India the most congenial soil. Wherever the Buddha went, he was followed by and surrounded not by non-Hindus, but by Hindus, those who were themselves saturated with the Vedic laws; but the Buddha's teaching like his heart was all-expanding and all-embracing and so it has survived his own body and swept across the face of the earth."[3]

The Buddha was not exclusive. He literally lived for humanity. His message was meant for all. He did not respect power or wealth. He was the first to rebel against the tyranny of the caste system. Buddhism was far too ethical to tolerate such hierarchical arrangement. The Buddha said, "As in the ocean all the great rivers lose their name and being, so in my doctrine all the castes merge."[4] The Buddha's order contained people of all castes. His message was that of human dignity and equality. Gandhi wrote, "The second thing that Gautama taught was that all that caste means today as it meant in his time also was wholly wrong. That is to say, he abolished every distinction of superiority and inferiority that was even in his time eating into the vitals of Hinduism."[5] The Dhammapada says, "Neither by matted hair, nor through his family, nor through birth is one a *brāhmaṇa.* In whom there exists truth and righteousness — pure is he, a *brāhmaṇa* is he."[6] Further: "By whom no evil is done through body, speech or mind, he who is restrained in these respects — him I call a *brāhmaṇa.*"[7]

The Buddha is so called because he realized the highest *bodhi* or spiritual illumination. Buddhism is both a system of exalted ethics and a way of spiritual realization. The spiritual experience of the Buddha is the basic source of the religious inspiration for Buddhists. The various Buddhist doctrines are derived and traced to the original experience of enlightenment of the Buddha. He shared with men and women the wealth of his experience. He therefore refused mere speculation on the nature of transcendent reality; nor was he interested in metaphysical discussions for their own sake. He saw that the greatest Vedic philosophers of his times interpreted the Upaniṣadic teachings in different ways; and the ordinary people were confused by most of them. He wanted to avoid a similar plight.

He was really concerned with providing practical remedies for the ills and sorrows of life. His teachings, therefore, were simple, direct, and practical. He emphasized the importance of securing peace and happiness through a strenuous moral life. Each individual has to attain the highest by his own effort. Whosoever attains purity attains *nirvāṇa*; it is the birthright of every human being. One has to assert his spirituality and to cultivate his inner life to achieve liberation. The Buddha insisted on right action, genuine morality, and love for humanity. Every individual has in him the potentiality and the possibility of securing the highest enlightenment through disciplined devotion in the pursuit of truth.

If by religion is meant faith in some supernatural Creator and a certain number of dogmas, the Buddha was certainly not a founder of such a religion. But what was originally only a reform movement soon came to be established as a distinctive religious tradition. Many of his followers in subsequent centuries deified him and reduced his teachings to new dogmas. And as dogmatic differences arose, Buddhism split itself into two branches, each claiming that it alone was loyal to the teachings of the Master. While Theravāda Buddhism placed its emphasis on individual attainment of salvation, Mahāyāna emphasized compassion for the redemption of humanity.

According to Mahāyāna Buddhism, the Buddha is to be adored as the Savior of men through the truth which he exemplified in his life. Further, the earthly Buddha is the eternal and Divine Buddha who reveals himself in all worlds. Thus, his followers glorified him almost as a Divine Being. The nature of the Godhead which was developed in the Mahāyāna is similar to that in Hinduism. *Dharmakāya* or the body of *Dharma* is the ultimate first principle, the Divine from which all things proceed and to which all return. It is not merely by human effort but by the grace of the Buddha that one attains *nirvāṇa*. This belief effectually freed Mahāyāna Buddhism from the charge of atheism.

Gandhi has made a pointed reference to what he considered as a misunderstanding of the position of the Buddha. To say that the Buddha taught atheism and nonexistence of the soul is to misrepresent the position of the Buddha. "I have heard it contended times without number and I have read it in books also claiming to express the spirit of Buddhism that Buddha did not believe in God. In my humble opinion such a belief contradicts the very central fact of Buddha's teaching. In my humble opinion such a confusion has arisen over his rejection and just rejection of all the base things that passed in his generation under the name of God. He undoubtedly rejected the notion that a being called God could be actuated by malice and could repent His actions, and like the kings of the earth could possibly have favorites. His whole soul rose in mighty indignation against the belief that a being called God required for His satisfaction the living blood of animals who were His own creation. He therefore reinstated God in the right place and dethroned the usurper who for the time being seemed to occupy the white throne. He emphasized and redeclared the eternal and unalterable existence of the moral government of this universe. He unhesitatingly said that the Law was

God Himself. God's Laws are eternal and unalterable and not separate from God Himself. It is an indispensable condition of His very perfection. And hence, the great confusion that Buddha disbelieved in God and simply believed in the moral law."[8]

Even the ideal of *nirvāṇa* is very far from being a kind of nothingness or total extinction, as it is often misinterpreted by certain scholars. *Nirvāṇa* is a positive condition; but because it is beyond the normal range of human thought, negative terms are often used to describe it. Buddhism is most certainly not a doctrine of life-negation. In Buddhism the objective is twofold : on the one side there is a need to emancipate our personality from the grip of forces that are selfish or self-centered and partly subconscious and unconscious; this is the negative aspect. It implies the extinction of all craving, resentment, and covetousness. It has also, on the other side, a positive aspect; it is the need of the human personality to find its fullest expression in the love of the Infinite, in compassion for all creatures, and to be identified with them and thus to find the ultimate freedom and salvation. The conception of *nirvāṇa* emphasizes this double aspect.

*Nirvāṇa* is not the annihilation of the soul, but the annihilation of its finiteness and the consequent enrichment of the personality being emptied of all selfishness and the realization of its unity and identity with the final Reality. It is the release from the "rounds of births and deaths". *Nirvāṇa* is not therefore death but eternal life. In the words of Gandhi, "*Nirvāṇa* is undoubtedly not utter extinction. So far as I have been able to understand the central fact of Buddha's life, *nirvāṇa* is utter extinction of all that is base in us, all that is corrupt and corruptible in us. *Nirvāṇa* is not like the black dead peace of the grave, but the living peace, the living happiness of a soul which is conscious of itself, and conscious of having its own abode in the heart of the eternal."[9] *Nirvāṇa* relates to the world of freedom, to the subject which transcends the object, and to the center of being. When the Buddha asks us to seek liberation and strive for it, he affirms the reality of another level of existence. He tells us that it is possible for us to overcome the time process and attain enlightenment by following *aṣṭāṅga mārga*, the Noble Eightfold Path.

Since the Noble Eightfold Path is recommended as a cure for the misery of life, *nirvāṇa* cannot be mere nothingness. Our moral practices are intended to rid life of its evils and make it worth living. If at all we are exhorted to be moral, it must be for the good of humankind; to be moral is to give a positive content to life. While morality implies assertion of life, its end cannot be negative. Since *nirvāṇa* is the final fruition of life, it cannot be nothingness.

This conclusion forces itself on a dispassionate student of the Buddha's teaching : "The destruction of greed, the destruction of hate, the destruction of illusion — this, O friend, is what is called *nibbāna.*" In other words, *nirvāṇa* does imply extinction not of life but of lust, ill-will, ignorance, anger, fear, and everything that makes life a burden. According to the noted Buddhist scholar Mrs. Rhys Davids, *nirvāṇa* implies mental enlightenment, mastery of self, and control of mind. The Upaniṣadic peace and joy are there. It also sees the end of the cycle of births and deaths. Therefore Buddhist *nirvāṇa* is nothing but Upaniṣadic *Mokṣa,* with a different emphasis and a different approach.

Immortality of the soul is one of the cardinal principles of all theistic religions. The teaching of the Buddha in this regard is unique. It is of course true that the Buddha denied the existence of a self or soul in the narrow sense of the word. He realized that before a man could love others as himself, he must first of all be convinced that this narrow self is not the real self and that it is to be overcome, subdued, and spiritualized. Further, the Buddha accepted the Upaniṣadic teaching of *skandhas* comprising the body, feeling, conceptual knowledge, tendencies, and lastly consciousness. But to maintain that the Buddha denied the immortal and unborn Supreme Spirit would be wholly inaccurate. For he frequently implies this Self or Spirit when he says, "*na me so atta*" (That is not myself), referring to the body and the empirical consciousness. A statement of the Hindu philosopher Śaṁkara is particularly relevant in this connection; he says, "Whenever we deny something unreal, it is with reference to something real." Further, if the doctrine of transmigration of the soul as expounded by Buddha should have any meaning, some sort of unity must be presupposed. There are also passages in which the Buddha has exhorted his followers, "Take refuge in the Self." As Mrs. Rhys Davids has pointed out, the Buddha is a critic of Brahminism in external matters, but its "internal system of spiritual values" is taken for granted by him.

It is not only unfortunate but utterly misleading that some scholars have said that the Buddha's teaching is pessimistic. If we interpret his words correctly, they are not pessimistic at all. He did say that everything can cause suffering; every phase of life can result in disharmony for a person. But suffering is for him only a matter of being out of harmony with life. He also proposes a remedy which is practical and ethical, and herein consists the Buddha's originality. In fact he taught only two things : suffering and release from suffering. Suffering ceases with complete cessation of craving and the cultivation of poise based on the "Middle Path."

The Buddha found around him cruelty and violence masquerading in the name of religion. The teaching of love and the practice of cruelty did not fit with each other. The Buddha wanted men to purify their hearts and give up violence; he propagated compassion and love. He revolutionized the concept of *ahiṁsā* by his rational approach. He laid exclusive emphasis on purity of motive. Sir Charles Eliot is of the opinion that the Hinduism of the present day owes to Buddhism the doctrine of the sanctity of animal life and the rejection of animal sacrifices. The Buddha insisted upon the necessity of cleansing the mind of base instincts and impulses. He did not attach undue importance to outward practices but wanted men to be free from greed, anger, and self-glorification. He enriched and elevated the concept of *ahiṁsā* by making it the outcome of love and compassion. It became a positive virtue and not a negative attitude.

The Buddha recognized a diversity of ways to reach the truth. But when the truth is attained the ways pass away. Both in theory and in practice, Buddhism has been one of the most broad-based of religions. In Japan, for instance, most people are at the same time following Buddhist and Shinto practices. The Buddha's approach is rational and empirical. Therefore the Buddhist philosophy of life and code of conduct appeal to the modern man deeply influenced by science. Its insistence on spiritual values and its ethic of love make it extremely attractive to people throughout the world. The Buddha insisted that his words should be accepted only after being tested both in theory and in practice. He wanted people not to rely on some external authority but to make their own self their support. He held that dependence on authority or on others, however exalted they may be, is against the law of spiritual development. Each man is the maker of his own destiny.

Buddhist religion and literature and art have ennobled and elevated a large part of humanity. During the expansion of Buddhism, it absorbed with great flexibility the traditions and cultures of the different countries which accepted its message. While adopting the beliefs and practices of indigenous cultures, it helped to reform and elevate them. Buddhism spread over the whole of Asia without shedding a single drop of blood. The German scholar Dr. Winternitz maintains that the conquest of human souls all over Asia by Buddhism is the only conquest of the spirit without violence in all history. Buddhism has adherents throughout southern and eastern Asia, and the brotherhood of Buddhists is one of the great unifying forces of the world. If spiritual values are not to disappear under the pressure of materialistic thought, Buddhism may well provide a powerful corrective.

### (iii) CHRISTIANITY

The supreme sacrifice of Jesus Christ on the cross for the redemption of humanity has been an unfailing source of inspiration through the ages. And where it has remained true to his central message of love, the religion that resulted from his sacrifice has wielded the same inspiration. In the early history of Christianity, the ideal of strict monasticism and wholehearted absorption in God was emphasized, though comparatively few were able to put it into practice. On the whole, the best Christian endeavor in recent times has been inspired by the idea of bettering humanity so as to establish the Kingdom of God on earth. This has been its chief strength among non-Christians. In India, the Sermon on the Mount and the figure of Jesus Christ have found a ready and warm response in the minds and hearts of the people and have become part of the Indian cultural heritage. Christ's life reaches the depths of the

Indian mind. Gandhi, himself, absorbed the New Testament's teaching, though he found no reason at all to change his religious allegiance. He was impressed by Christ's example as a way of life. And Christianity's compassion for the common people and insistence on the service of society, as well as preference for the humble and the poor, made a strong appeal to him. But as ecclesiastical dogma and theological speculation, it did not make the same appeal.

Gandhi also felt that Christianity as generally practiced in the West was not in line with the true spirit of Jesus's teaching. Although Christianity originated as a gentle and self-abnegating creed, it was transformed by about the fourth century A.D. into an aggressive and proselytizing religion in which even war was sanctioned, if not encouraged by the Church. No doubt it made possible the emergence of a number of sublime saints. But the medieval ages in Europe witnessed an almost imperial sway on the part of the Christian Church, which did not always exemplify the gentle and godlike way of life of Jesus. He wondered whether the message of Jesus had been understood in its true spirit by many of his professed followers. Gandhi thought that the proliferation of mutually competing and sometimes opposing churches and denominations had taken the fire out of Christianity. And he felt that some of the Western Christian traditional practices and conventions in modern times needed serious rethinking. He said, "The cross undoubtedly makes a universal appeal the moment you give it a universal meaning, in place of the narrow one that is often heard at ordinary meetings; but then you have to have the eyes of the soul with which to contemplate it."[1]

Gandhi rediscovered for himself the simple and sublime religion of Jesus in the course of his search for truthful spiritual living. In his interpretation of the Gospels, he paid the highest reverence to the quality of Jesus's life. He found the symbol and center of true Christianity in the cross. To him the New Testament was not a textbook of theology; it was a revelation of the meaning of eternity and of the life of spirit.

Advising Indian Christians, he said, "I consider Western Christianity in its practical working a negation of Christ's Christianity. I cannot conceive Jesus, if he was living in the flesh in our midst, approving of modern Christian organizations, public worship, or modern ministry. If Indian Christians will simply cling to the Sermon on the Mount, which was delivered not merely to peaceful disciples but to a groaning world, they would not go wrong, and they would find that no religion is false, and if all lived according to their likes and in the fear of God, they would not need to worry about organizations, forms of worship, and ministry. The Pharisees had all that, but Jesus would have none of it, for they were using their office as a cloak for hypocrisy and worse. Cooperation with the forces of good and non-cooperation with the forces of evil are the two things we need for a good and pure life, whether it is called Hindu, Muslim or Christian." He adds, "The message of Jesus as I understand it is contained in his Sermon on the Mount, unadulterated and taken as a whole; and even in connection with the Sermon on the Mount, my own interpretation of the message is different from the orthodox. The message, to my mind, has suffered distortion in the West. It may be presumptuous for me to say so, but as a devotee of truth, I should not hesitate to say what I feel."[2]

Gandhi was not prepared to accept the doctrine of vicarious atonement as was presented to him. He could not believe that one's sins could be expiated through the sufferings of someone else. He found no basis for the theory that moral responsibility is transferable. The very idea appeared to him to be contrary to moral law. He also saw a subtle danger in it leading to irresponsibility in the conduct of human beings. He said, "I do not seek redemption from the consequences of my sin. I seek redemption from sin itself, or rather from the very thought of sin. Until I have attained that end, I shall be content to be restless."[3] Jesus explicitly told Nicodemus (John 3:3-5) that the individual could only be saved by means of self-purification or regeneration by being reborn of water (total purification) and of the spirit (divine knowledge). Gandhi, like Jesus himself, chose to meet evil courageously but nonviolently. He was of the opinion that no man can escape responsibility for his commissions and omissions, as he was told in South Africa, by merely taking resort to worship. Moreover, to say, "This was right for him, but it would be wrong for me," is to tear up those parts of Jesus's teachings in which he bade men follow his example and do his works.

Gandhi shared the view of Jesus regarding God's love for humanity and the entire creation. All things are derived from one Spirit. That is why Jesus practiced the spiritual law of *ahiṁsā* and never compromised in the application of non-violence. All true followers of Jesus, according to Gandhi, must learn not only to refrain from hatred but should overcome evil and hate with love and goodwill. Jesus himself had the faith to believe that his death on the cross would prove a mightier weapon for the vindication of truth than all the conquering armies of empires. Truth must be its own vindication. Jesus Christ chose to meet evil unarmed and unafraid and readily bore all its wounds. Following Jesus, Gandhi could never understand or appreciate the employment of violence and war in the name of religion.

In Christianity, belief in certain dogmas and doctrines is considered essential. Its appeal usually has been : "Believe and ye shall be saved." In the words of Kenneth C. Barnes, "The Church, for all its claims to divine guidance, is a human institution and has shown the contradiction and paradox present in human institutions. It has lived in unceasing tension between the urge to discipline and dominate the Christian community, and the impulse to reach intimacy with God, an experience that takes a man beyond rules to the point where he can say with St Augustine : 'Love God and do what you like.' Thus its greatest saints have walked on a razor's edge between orthodoxy and arch-heresy." He adds, "It is saddening to recognize how the Church in its organization rapidly and thoroughly took over most of these attitudes of the Scribes and Pharisees that Jesus so fiercely condemned. However broadly the doctrine might be interpreted, practice and rule sought to imprison God within the organization, and the wind of the spirit which for Jesus 'bloweth where it listeth' could be felt only in ecclesiastical precincts. One result has been that even today many believers, and even half-believers cannot imagine God working outside the organization that the Church has provided for Him. In practice they severely limit the omnipotence they accord to God in theory."[4]

Gandhi refused to subscribe to the view of the absolute uniqueness of Jesus Christ as the only-begotten Son of God or that Christianity is the only true religion and that the Bible is the only true revelation. He saw the need for the reconciliation of Christianity with other religions. In fact, he found in the great religions of the world many points of similarity. For example, in the matter of renunciation, otherworldliness, and inner perfection, Christianity was not, according to him, different from other religions. He firmly believed that the concept of the antithesis between Christianity and the other great religions was false and should go. He held that Christians *alone* can never be the chosen people nor the Christian Church the *only* Church of God. To say so, or to believe in such a doctrine, is to deny that God Himself is the Father and Redeemer of all. Gandhi often said that no religion had a monopoly of truth or salvation. He would rather say with St Paul, "As many as are led by the Spirit of God, they are the sons of God."[5] Gandhi maintained, "If Jesus was like God, or God Himself, then all men were like God and could be God Himself. My reason was not ready to believe literally that Jesus by his death and by his blood redeemed the sins of the world. Metaphysically there might be some truth to it. Again, according to Christianity only human beings had souls, and not other living beings, for whom death meant complete extinction, while I held a contrary belief. I could accept Jesus as a martyr, an embodiment of sacrifice and a divine teacher, but not as the most perfect man ever born. His death on the cross was a great example to the world, but that there was anything like a mysterious or miraculous virtue in it my heart could not accept. The pious lives of Christians did not give me anything that the lives of other faiths had failed to give me. I had seen in other lives just the same reformation that I had heard among Christians. Philosophically, there was nothing extraordinary in Christian principles. From the point of view of sacrifice, it seemed to me that the Hindus greatly surpassed Christians. It was impossible for me to regard Christianity as a perfect religion or the greatest of all religions."[6]

Gandhi was not prepared to accept the dogma that Jesus is the only Son of God. In his words, "I do not take as literally true the text that Jesus is the only-begotten Son of God. God cannot be an exclusive Father and I cannot ascribe exclusive divinity to Jesus. He is as divine as Krishṇa or Rāma or Muhammad or Zoroaster. Similarly I do not regard every word of the Bible as the inspired word of God even as I do not regard every word of the Vedas or the Koran as inspired. The sum total of each of these books is certainly inspired. But I miss that inspiration in many of the things taken individually. The Bible is as much a book of religion with me as the Gītā and the Koran." He adds, "I would also dispute the claim that Christianity is the only true religion. It is also a true religion, a noble religion, and along with other religions it has contributed to raise the moral height of mankind. But it has yet to make a greater contribution. After all, what is 2,000 years in the life of a religion ? Just now, Christianity comes to mankind in a tainted form. Fancy bishops supporting slaughter in the name of Christianity !"[7]

Gandhi was aware that a considerable section of Christians held the view that Christianity was the fulfillment of all other religions. According to them it was possible to arrange religions in a hierarchical order with Christianity as the "crown" of other religions. All religions are attempts to meet the fundamental religious needs and aspirations of human beings everywhere; but Christianity is unique and final. Totalitarian claims of this type, in one sense or another, are made by several religions. No matter by which religion such a claim is made, it betrays the same kind of pride, self-righteousness, and insensitivity, and a desire for authority over their respective followers; it is the pride of possessing the ultimate truth or dogma. But Gandhi maintained that no religion could stand in judgment on another. He refused to judge the degree of divinity of prophets or to make invidious comparisons between religions. On being questioned whether he would not consider Christ as being more divine than other prophets Gandhi answered, "No. For the simple reason that we have no data. Historically we have more data about Muhammad than anyone else because he was more recent in time. For Jesus there are less data, and still less for Buddha, Rāma, and Krishṇa. And when we know so little about them, it is preposterous to say that one of them was more divine than another. In fact, even if a great deal of data were available, no judge should shoulder the burden of sifting all the evidence, if only for this reason that it requires a highly spiritual person to gauge the degree of divinity of the subjects he examines. To say that Jesus was ninety-nine per cent divine and Muhammad was fifty per cent divine and Krishṇa was ten per cent is to arrogate to oneself a function which really does not belong to man."[8]

Moreover, the spiritual truths taught by prophets and sages are matters of profound experience; they are internal and qualitative. Such experiences can never be compared or judged. The realizations of the Buddha or Christ or Muhammad are matters of faith to their respective followers. They are all equally precious to the followers of the religions concerned. Hence, spiritual truths which are qualitative in character cannot be measured or arranged in a hierarchy representing less or more truth. Besides, organized religions, which generally function at a less exalted level, cannot claim perfection; they have wielded enormous power, and it seems all of them are guilty of the cardinal sin of pride. It must be remembered though that the purpose of every religion is not to glorify itself but to help its followers to know God and be one with Him. In this light, every religion can be of help to every other religion in the common pursuit of truth. Religions can be complementary and supplementary to one another. This does not, of course, mean displacement of any religion by any other. The great religions must help one another in fulfilling themselves. Such a true fellowship of religions may broaden, deepen, and enrich every religion. Each religion has its own distinct message or particular stress or emphasis. Because of these things, it is difficult to support the claim of certain Christian theologians that the good elements of all religions are crowned in the Christian revelation. Such a claim shows a sort of blindness to the spiritual treasures of other religions. It means that every other religion is either inadequate or even false. But, as a matter of fact, a generally acceptable criterion for such a judgment does not exist and has not been laid down. It is questionable whether anyone outside a particular faith can really judge that faith. Bias and ignorance vitiate one's judgments of other religions. As Hocking says, "It would certainly be a matter of shame rather than congratulation if the only evidence for the finality of our faith were its supernatural origin and the only evidence for its supernatural origin were our faith."[9]

Actually, for Christians to ignore the spiritual values in other religions is to be blind to some of Christianity's own basic concepts, which it shares with other religions. Professor W. C. Smith considers that it is unchristian to think that Christianity is the only true religion and the others are either false or insufficient. He fervently appeals : "May I plead that we abandon, as utterly unworthy, the traditional notion that if Christianity is true, then it must follow that other faiths are false — or at least inadequate. This entire formulation seems to me inept; the ideas juxtaposed just do not cohere. ... For the moment, let me point out some ways in which such a position gets one tied up in unchristian knots. For example, there is danger of the converse proposition : that if anyone else's faith turns out to be valid or adequate, then it would follow that Christianity must be false — a form of logic that has, in tact, driven many from their own faiths, and indeed from any faith at all. If one's chances of getting to Heaven — or to use a now-a-days more acceptable metaphor, of coming into God's presence — are dependent upon other people's not getting there, then one becomes walled up within the quite intolerable position that the Christian has a vested interest in other men's damnation. It is shocking to admit it, but this actually takes place. When an observer comes back from Asia, or from a study of Asian religious traditions, and reports that contrary to accepted theory some Hindus and Buddhists and some Muslims lead a pious and moral life and seem very near to God by any possible standard, so that as one can see in these particular cases at least, faith is as 'adequate' as Christian faith, then presumably a Christian should be overjoyed, enthusiastically hopeful that this be true, even though he may be permitted a fear lest it be not so. Instead, I have sometimes witnessed just the opposite : an emotional resistance to the news, one hoping firmly that it is not so though perhaps with a covert fear that it might be. Whatever the rights and wrongs of the situation theoretically, I submit that this is just not Christian, and is indeed not tolerable. It will not do, to have a faith that can be undermined by God's saving one's neighbor; or to be afraid lest other men turn out to be closer to God than one has been led to suppose."[10]

According to Gandhi, love and service are the two characteristic features of the Christian way of life. Everyone should aspire to live up to these ideals in everyday life. It is not at all harmful to one's own religion to sit at the feet of the holy men of other religions and to learn from them. On the other hand, such conduct adds to the fullness and depth of one's own religious experience. Gandhi looked upon the founders of religions as great teachers and saints and men of great spiritual stature who showed people the proper path to God according to the needs of the times and circumstances. They were all benefactors of mankind. He made no distinction between them, and held all of them in great reverence. He was eager to recognize the spiritual truths and insights of other faiths which were only too evident to him. He conceded that the saints and sages of other religions had also heard the call of God. He realized the great necessity of cooperation among the followers of the great religions. He stressed the need for a clearer understanding of the meaning of religious tolerance, mutual reverence among religions, and religious freedom, which the sacred scriptures of all religions are concerned to defend. He realized the necessity of fellowship with persons of other religions in order to cultivate lasting ties of community in the deeper levels of the spirit. He saw the importance of all spiritual forces joining together in the face of threats from scientism, technology, materialism, and nuclear annihilation.

The Bible itself supports the position that God has been speaking through ages to those who have not held the Biblical faith. Such passages as : "Truly I perceive that God shows no partiality, but in every nation, any one who fears him and does what is right is acceptable to Him" (Acts 10:34-35). "He did not leave Himself without a witness" (Acts 14:17). There are also individuals in other religions who show evidence that they are near the Kingdom of God. How can anyone say that God, the Maker and the Father of all men, who "shows no partiality" and to whom all human beings are dear, has not made Himself known to the people of Japan and India as He had made Himself known to the people of Palestine? Can it be maintained that the majority of mankind which does not profess the Christian faith has been deprived of divine communication ?

As they learn more regarding such personalities as Zoroaster, Buddha, and Muhammad, thoughtful Christians are beginning to review their traditional attitudes to other faiths. In order to establish the uniqueness of the revelation in Jesus Christ, it is not necessary to decry the relevance and significance of other religions. Is it not necessary for every religious person to understand what God is doing in and through other religions? Should not the interpretation of God's activities be big enough to include Him in every religion, wherever truth, goodness, and love operate?

Gandhi was aware of a growing acceptance in certain sections of the Christian community of the need to get into real contact with the votaries of other religions, as fellow pilgrims seeking truth and the good life. He commended the growing spirit of tolerance among them : "It is a matter of pleasure to me to be able to say that, if I have had painful experiences of Christians and Christian missionaries, I have had pleasant ones also which I treasure. There is no doubt that among them the spirit of toleration is growing. Among individuals there is also a deeper study of Hinduism and other faiths and an appreciation that the other great faiths of the world are not false. One is thankful for the growing liberal spirit, but I have the conviction that much still remains to be done in that direction."[11]

Gandhi maintained that people of all religions have a deep interest in Christ. As he pointed out, Hindus hail the claim of Jesus that "I and the Father are one" (John 10:30). Some Buddhists have spoken of him as the Buddha of the West. The Koran speaks of Jesus as the Messiah, as a prophet and messenger of God. All this should provide a basis for a two-way communication and spiritual fellowship between Christianity and the other great religions.

Gandhi interpreted Christ's work not in an exclusive but in a comprehensive sense. That was his way to credit Christ with universality and humanity. He wanted everyone to employ his own profound insight and deepest need in the interpretation of the cross. Thus, Christ would become meaningful and universal and a perpetual inspiration to men in all times and places. In the words of Gandhi, "If Jesus came to earth again, he would disown many things that are being done in the name of Christianity. It is not he who says, 'Lord, Lord' but 'He that doeth the will of the Lord' (Mt. 7:21) that is a true Christian. And cannot he who has not heard the name of Jesus Christ do the will of the Lord ?"[12]

### (iv) ISLAM

The essentials of Islam are : first, a passionate belief in the One God without a second, and second, utter subservience of the human will to the Divine Will, accepting Him as the Creator of the Universe, full of power and mercy and goodness. The belief in prophets is strictly subsidiary. The Koran states that the great prophets of different religions like Judaism and Christianity must be accepted and revered. Gandhi said, "I certainly regard Islam as one of the inspired religions, and therefore the Holy Koran as an inspired book and Muhammad as one of the prophets."[1] The austere life and profound teachings of Prophet Muhammad influenced Gandhi a great deal. According to C. F. Andrews, "His [Gandhi's] profound admiration for the character of Prophet Muhammad, as a man of faith and action, and also for his son-in-law Ali, as a man of tender love and suffering, deeply affected him. He was impressed to a remarkable degree by the nobility of the early Caliphate and the fervent faith of the first followers of the Prophet. The bare simplicity with which they lived, their chivalrous devotion to the poor, their intense belief in God's overruling majesty, all these things had a great effect upon him."[2] He added, "Following the example of the Prophet of Islam, Mahatma Gandhi has never for a moment separated the political from the spiritual, or failed to deal directly with the social evils which stood out before his eyes. Thus the Prophet's supreme, practical instinct as a reformer, combined with his intense faith in God as the sole Creator and Director of the Universe, has been a source of constant strength and support to Mahatma Gandhi himself, in his own struggle. ... Whenever Mahatma Gandhi has turned from this political aspect of the struggle in order to gain strength for the great conception of suffering injury without retaliation, he has constantly taken the character of the Prophet's son-in-law Ali, and of Hassan and Hussain for his example. The story of the suffering of these descendants of the Prophet ... is indeed full of pathos. It illustrates ... 'the irresistible might of meekness,' which has always appealed most to Mahatma

Gandhi. ... Mahatma Gandhi in his writings often refers to the early days of the Prophet's mission, when he was despised and rejected by his own countrymen and was fain to submit to every form of humiliation in silence. ... Thus in his own way he has found the teaching of the Prophet of Islam fully compatible with the principle of *ahiṁsā*, or nonviolence, whereon he lays such stress."[3]

Gandhi rejected the theory that the rise of Islam was a triumph of fanaticism over tolerant principles and that it spread through the sword. He considered that its phenomenal success was due to its revolutionary principles, and its ability to lead the masses out of the hopeless situation created by the decay of ancient civilizations. In fact, Islam was welcomed as a deliverer by oppressed peoples. Though Islam started as a militant religion, its militancy softened after the Christian crusades and continued until the revival of its militancy in the modern period in India and the Middle East. Islam remained comparatively a religion of peace. In the words of Gandhi, "My association with the noblest of Mussalmans has taught me to see that Islam has spread not by the power of the sword, but by the prayerful love of an unbroken line of its saints and fakirs. Warrant there is in Islam for drawing the sword; but the conditions laid down are so strict that they are not capable of being fulfilled by everybody. Where is the unerring General to order Jehad ? Where is the suffering and love and purification that must precede the very idea of drawing the sword ?... We are too imperfect and impure and selfish, as yet, to resort to an armed conflict in the name of God."[4] Muslim fanaticism and militancy, wherever they may be found, are in open defiance of the noble teachings of the Prophet Muhammad and have unfortunately been recurrent features of Muslim conquest in all lands. There is nothing in the Koran to warrant the use of force in conversion. The Holy Book expresses in clearest language possible : "There is no compulsion in religion." According to Gandhi, "The Prophet's whole life is a repudiation of compulsion in religion. No Mussalman has to my knowledge ever approved of compulsion. Islam would cease to be a world religion if it were to rely upon force for its propagation. Secondly, historically speaking, the charge of conversion by force cannot be proved against its followers as a body. And whenever attempts have been made to convert by force responsible Mussalmans have repudiated such conversions."[5]

A unique spirit of brotherhood and comradeship pervades the teachings of Islam. Etymologically Islam means peace, peace with God by recognizing and paying homage to His Oneness, and peace on earth with neighbors. Muhammad affirms the unity of God and brotherhood of man. The predominant note in Islam is the belief in One God with name but without form, and the discipline prescribed to attain the highest is the path of surrender and devotion. Islam like any other religion was the product of the times and of the surroundings in which it flourished. Gandhi maintains, "I do regard Islam to be a religion of peace in the same sense as Christianity, Buddhism, and Hinduism are. No doubt there are differences in degree, but the object of all these religions is peace. I know the passages that can be quoted from Koran to the contrary. But so is it possible to quote passages from Vedas to the contrary. ... I have given my opinion that the followers of Islam are too free with the sword. But that is not due to the teaching of the Koran. That is due, in my opinion, to the environment in which Islam was born."[6]

The laws of the Koran revolutionized social relations. Theologically, also, Islam exercised a liberalizing influence. It maintained that all apostles of God who lived before the Prophet Muhammad, irrespective of their places and ages of advent, were great and holy. It encouraged toleration, sympathy, and understanding for the habits, views, and faiths of others. The Koran proclaims, "And certainly we raised in every nation a messenger saying: Serve Allah and shun the devil."[7] Further, "And we sent no messenger but with the language of his people, so that he might explain to them clearly."[8] Hence Islam ushered in an era of cosmopolitanism and spirituality. Historically, Islam rose as a protest against religious persecution and as a refuge for the oppressed. It fought rigid rites and rituals, dogmatism, and hypocrisy. Religious life was in a state of confusion in Arabia, Persia, Mesopotamia, Syria, Palestine, and Egypt. God had disappeared in a crowd of angels, saints, and apostles. Hence the new cry of Islam : "There is but one God". That was the anchor of a simple faith in the stormy sea of religious and moral disintegration.

Muhammad with great foresight and insight readily granted to his Christian subjects security of their persons, freedom of trade, ownership of their goods, and toleration of their worship. This principle of toleration was kept up strictly not only by the immediate successors of the Prophet but over the whole period of Arabic ascendancy. When Jerusalem was defeated by the Khalif Omar, the inhabitants of the vanquished city were left in possession of their worldly goods and were allowed freedom of worship. A special quarter of the city was allotted as the residence of the Christian population with their Patriarch and the clergy.

Mahatma Gandhi found in the Koran progressive social principles and admirable codes of personal behavior. Muhammad did not engage in vain metaphysics, but applied himself to improving social conditions among his people by regulations concerning cleanliness, sobriety, fasting, and prayer. He esteemed almsgiving and charity. With great vision and liberality, he accepted the possibility of salvation for men of any form of faith provided they were virtuous and good. Islam also encouraged learning and cultivation of the intellect. The works of the sages of ancient Greece were rescued, collected, and preserved by the Arabs. They translated the Greek classics and transmitted them to the West, thereby making possible the Renaissance. Islam absorbed the strong points of the older religions. The centers of Islam were those very historical regions where the older civilizations of the Egyptians, Syrians, Jews, Persians, and Greeks had risen and fallen. The new religion spread fast in Arabia and in the Persian Empire. It achieved tremendous vogue in Africa and is acknowledged as a great civilizing force in the history of humanity.

No claim is made in Islam that its founder is divine. This denial of divinity to the Prophet has made Islam one of the purest monotheistic religions. Once divinity is conceded to a Prophet, he very soon assumes the attributes of the Supreme Being. Further, the Arabs for the first time conceived, in that part of the world, the sublime idea of the common origin of religions. All religions, accordingly, were so many efforts of the human mind to solve the great mysteries of life and nature. The Koran declares, "Say: We believe in Allah and that which is revealed unto us and that which is revealed unto Abraham and Ishmael and Isaac and Jacob and the tribes and that which was vouchsafed unto Moses and Jesus and the prophets from their Lord. We make no distinction between any one of them, and unto Him we have surrendered."[9] Muhammad thought of himself as one who purified the ancient faith and rid it of the extravagances that had crept into it. The Koran proclaims, "The same religion has he established for you that he enjoined on Noah, which we have by inspiration sent to thee, and that he enjoined on Abraham, Moses, and Jesus, namely, that you should remain steadfast in religion and make no divisions therein."[10] As all religions have the common mission of the spiritual upliftment of humanity, the doctrines and dogmas peculiar to each should not prevent the realization of the spiritual unity of mankind.

In India, the rise of reformers like Kabir, Nanak, Tukaram, Chaitanya, and others, who brought about a popular revolt against Brāhminical orthodoxy and authoritarianism was to a great extent promoted by the social impact of Islam. Islam did not fail to impart to Hinduism some of its monotheistic zest. And conversely, the pure monotheism of Islam has not been wholly able to withstand the influence of symbols and images, and hence the tombs of pirs, or saints, are far more common in India than in other Muslim lands. Yet with all this mutual give and take, Hinduism and Islam stand today in South Asia as two opposing forces more conscious of their differences than of their similarity. The task of reconciliation attempted by Gandhi is yet to be completed. It is yet to be realized that these two religions are neither contradictory nor hostile but complementary to one another. There are differences, of course. But they are to be understood sympathetically and appreciated. It is fanatics who exploit them to create rifts and conflicts. Actually, knowledge of Islam's contribution would shake the Hindus out of their complacency on the one hand and, on the other, cure the exclusive fanaticism of the Muslims of our day by bringing them face to face with the true spirit of the faith they profess. In the words of Gandhi, "I have striven for Hindu-Muslim unity because India cannot live free without it, and because we would both deny God if we considered one another as natural enemies."[11]

## (v) THE PROBLEM OF HINDU-MUSLIM UNITY

Very early in life, Gandhi envisaged one of the great problems of India, namely, the unity of Hindus and Muslims. He wondered how children of one God and one land could raise barriers that kept their hearts apart. With the means of truth and love ("nonviolence", as he called it), he sought to break down these barriers, and left behind him the message of his life and death. His example serves as a continuous reservoir of inspiration to those who wish to rise above differences of creed and caste and barren polemics. He said, "This unity among all is no new love with me. I have treasured it, acted up to it, from my youth upward. When I went to London as a mere lad in 1889, I believed in it as passionately as I do now. When I went to South Africa in 1893, I worked it out in every detail of my life. Love so deep-seated as it is in me will not be sacrificed even for the realm of the whole world."[1] He found enormous waste of energy in religious bigotry. He felt that both Hindus and Muslims had gone wrong and both had failed to realize God. The whole spectacle made him sad : "We may think we are living, but disunited we are worse than dead. The Hindu thinks that in quarreling with the Mussalman he is benefiting Hinduism, and the Mussalman thinks that in fighting Hindus he is benefiting Islam. But each is ruining his faith."[2]

Hindus and Muslims of India fail to recognize their kinship because they still envisage Rāma as a tribal God who is expected to be partial to Hindus, and Allah as a tribal God who protects only the followers of Islam and has nothing but blood and iron for the rest of the world. Gandhi said that Īśvara and Allah are but different names of the same Universal Father; that Rāma does not need costly pilgrimages nor is Allah disturbed by music before the mosques. But both orthodox Hindus and Muslims considered Gandhi and his followers to be mistaken. Gandhi expressed his view as follows : "Divided we must ever be slaves. This unity therefore cannot be a mere policy to be discarded when it does not suit us.... Hindu-Muslim unity must be our creed to last for all time under all circumstances."[3]

Gandhi worked and prayed for the day when Hindu and

Muslim, in temple and mosque, would sing together and live in friendship and peace. He left no stone unturned to achieve this end. He threw himself into the struggle to heal the breach between the two communities. "I am striving to become the best cement between the two communities. My longing is to be able to cement the two with my blood, if necessary."[4] It pained him to see that men were delighted to revile one another in the name of God. He complained that they lacked the sympathy to be able to understand one another. As he explained, "Say Īśvara, say Khuda or Allah—it is all one." He asked, "What can be more natural than that Hindus and Muslims, born and bred in India and having the same adversaries, the same hopes, should be permanent friends, brothers born of the same Mother India ? The surprise is that we should fight, not that we should unite."[5] To Gandhi, Hindu-Muslim unity consisted "in our having a common purpose, a common goal, and common sorrows. It is best promoted by cooperating with each other to reach the common goal, by sharing one another's sorrow and by mutual toleration."[6]

Part of the unpleasantness between the two communities seems to have been due to the fact that Muslims came to India as invaders. The chief object of the early foreign conquerors who happened to be Muslims was to convert the infidels or "to send them to hell with the sword."[7] And the early hostility towards the invaders seems to have been carried over to the present day. But India had happy contacts with Islam long before the Muslim invasions began. Islam as a religion is not responsible for the cruel excesses of some of its followers. But, on the whole, ignorance of the deep cultural elements of each other's religion has kept Hindus and Muslims psychologically and culturally apart. Yet as Gandhi has explained, "For good or for ill, the two communities are wedded to India; they are neighbors, sons of the same soil, they are destined to die here as they are born here. Nature will force them to live in peace if they do not come together voluntarily."[8]

Gandhi held that it was incorrect to say that religion was responsible for the political conflicts between Hindus and Muslims. In fact, religion, in the genuine sense of the term, has not played any part, though the word has been much used in this connection. It is this phenomenon which in Idnia has come to be known as "communalism." Actually, it is one particular group or the other craving power and patronage that has played havoc with Indian national unity. Attempts were made again and again to solve this communal problem and restore peace and harmony between Hindus and Muslims. Gandhi was himself the foremost to seize every opportunity to promote good will and friendship between the two communities. But there was one fundamental difficulty. The ruling power (the British government) based its policy on the age-old Machiavellian principle of "Divide and Rule." It upset any real settlement between the two communities by alternately favoring one or the other. Even so, leaders held "Unity Conferences" from time to time. Sincere people on both sides tried for a settlement. The late Moulana Mahomed Ali convened a conference in Delhi in 1924 under the shadow of Gandhi's great fast for 21 days for the sake of Hindu-Muslim unity. Gandhi had earlier wholeheartedly supported the Muslims in their Khilafat campaign and had agitated for the release of the Ali brothers.

At one time it almost looked that communal harmony in India had been achieved. But fanatics on either side, encouraged by the alternating favors of the government, kept up the quarrel. And yet Gandhi did not lose heart : "Today though the Hindu-Muslim question wears an ugly face, it belongs very largely to the people, and there lies my hope for a permanent peace out of the present wanton violence. ... In 1920-21 we had just a passing glimpse of Hindu-Muslim unity as it would be when completely achieved. The effect can never vanish completely, though ugly elements which have come upon the surface may shake one's faith for the moment."[9]

Some of the wisest men and saints of both Islam and Hinduism teach the same things: faith in the oneness of God, the immortality of the soul, the ephemeral character of material things, and the eternal character of things spiritual. The Sufis and the Indian mystics derived inspiration from a common source: experience of the Divine in the human soul. Kabir, the religious poet and mystic saint of medieval India, sang: 'Hari is made to dwell in the East, Allah in the West. But seek Him in your heart. You will find there both Karim and

Rāma. If God is only in the mosque, to whom does the country outside belong ? Rāma is supposed to be in the pilgrim places and in His images. But they have found Him in neither yet. Who said that the Vedas and the book [the Koran are] false ? They are so to those who do not think. Within all bodies there is but One and no second. Man or woman, they are but Thy form. Kabir is but a child of Allah-Rāma and He is his Guru and Pir alike."[10] Even today many Hindus have the best of relations with Muslim divines. Hindus join in great numbers in the celebration of Muslim festivals like Muharram. And throughout the country Hindus and Muslims are living and working together in peace. But unfortunately the potential for conflict lies just beneath the surface.

A careful analysis will show that the real causes of Hindu-Muslim conflict have been more economic and political than religious. Actually, as independence began to appear to lie within the realm of possibility, each community became more and more greedy in its demands, and soon there was an ever-mounting communal tension. What both sides wanted was more posts in the government, more representation in legislatures, and more political power. One of the most important causes that widened the gulf between the Hindus and Muslims was the introduction of separate electorates by the British government. Though there was a demand for it, the demand was in fact instigated from above. Accordingly, Muslims could stand for election and be elected by a separate Muslim electorate and Hindus equally so. This was completely opposed to the process of unification and integration that had been going on silently in the country for centuries. The separate electorates created disruption, and barriers were created where none existed previously. The whole fabric of political and social life became vitiated and religion took on political overtones.

Communal riots became the order of the day. Every trifle was magnified and every little grudge or even differing religious practice became tremendously important. For long, cow sacrifice in India on the day of Bakrid was a source of discord between Hindus and Muslims. And whenever Hindu and Muslim festivals fell upon the same date there was the danger of the eruption of communal riots. Further, music before mosques became a constant source of friction breaking out in mob violence.

These difficulties, though complex and bitter, are not insurmountable. The psychological aspects of the problem would not be so difficult of resolution if people were less emotional. The problem is a challenge to the sagacity and broad-mindedness of all thinking people. In the opinion of Jawaharlal Nehru, "What was needed was good will and mutual consideration to avoid these disputes. A little adjustment on both sides would have brought about a reasonable settlement. But religious passions scarcely listen to the voice of reason."[11]

With the improvement of economic conditions and more and more opportunity for gainful employment, communal tension is sure to tone down. The safeguards incorporated in the Constitution of the Republic of India for minorities should go a long way to assuage the fear and sense of insecurity on the part of Muslims. More important is a social atmosphere which ensures good will for the minority community. The mutual exchange of ideas and services will further a friendly atmosphere. Every person and every community should look beyond their selfish interests and follow the higher ideals of their religious traditions. Competitive interests should be subordinated to one common purpose — the welfare of all. Common interests will create mutual consideration and make men and women realize that their own interests are involved in the interests of their neighbors.

It is through proper education that one learns to see his own good in the good of all. Once such education is available, communal tension is bound to decrease and cooperation between the followers of different religions in constructive and humanitarian activities will become easy and natural. Understanding leads to recognition of the good and valuable elements in others and their faiths. And in political affairs it will lead people to think in terms of the country as a whole and not in terms of religious sections or groups. The study of comparative religion by religious leaders and educators will help clear confusion and prejudice. People will learn to see things in the proper perspective. They will see that religion is not merely rites and ceremonies, but involves an inner spirit of harmony and good will. They will outgrow fanaticism and half-truths. It is only in such an atmosphere that real unity can emerge : "The true beauty of Hindu-Muslim unity lies in each remaining true to his own religion and yet being true to each other. For we are thinking of Hindus and Muslims even of the most orthodox type being able to regard one another as natural friends instead of regarding one another as natural enemies as they have done hitherto."[12]

**References**

(i) Hinduism

1. *Young India*, 24-11-1927.
2. *Ibid.*
3. *Young India*, 8-4-1926.
4. *Ibid.*, 29-9-1927.
5. S. Radhakrishnan, *The Hindu View of Life*, Macmillan Publishing Company, New York, 1973, p. 55.
6. *Ibid.*, p. 55.
7. *Ibid.*, p. 17.
8. *Ibid.*, p. 89.
9. *Young India*, 6-10-1921.
10. Jawaharlal Nehru, *Autobiography*, Allied Publishers, New Delhi, 1962.
11. *Young India*, 15-12-1927.
12. *Ibid.*, 6-10-1921.
13. *Ibid.*, 6-10-1921.
14. *Harijan*, 30-1-1937.
15. *Ibid.*, 30-1-1937.
16. *Ibid.*
17. *Ibid.*
18. *Bhagavadgītā*, VI. 30.
19. *Harijan*, 26-12-1936.
20. *Young India*, 8-6-1921.
21. *Ibid.*, 29-1-1925.
22. *Ibid.*, 15-12-1927.

(ii) Buddhism

1. *Young India*, 24-11-1927.
2.
3. *Ibid.*, 15-12-1927.
4. *Ibid.*, 24-11-1927.
5. Dhalke, P., *Buddhist Essays*, Macmillan and Company, London, 1908, p. 59.
6. *Young India*, 15-12-1927.
7. Dhammapada, XXVI : 393.
8. *Ibid.*, XXVI : 391.

9. *Young India*, 24-11-1927.
10. *Ibid.*, 24-11-1927.

(iii) CHRISTIANITY

1. M. K. Gandhi, *My Dear Child*, Navajivan Publishing House, Ahmedabad, 1956, p. 86.
2. *Young India*, 23-3-1926.
3. M. K. Gandhi, *op. cit.*, p. 104.
4. Kenneth C. Barnes, *The Creative Imagination*, Friends House, London, 1960, pp. 67-68.
5. Romans 8 : 14.
6. M. K. Gandhi, *op. cit.*, p. 170.
7. *Harijan*, 6-3-1937.
8. *Ibid.*, 6-3-1937.
9. William Earnest Hocking, *Living Religions And A World Faith*, Allen and Unwin, London, 1940.
10. Wilfred Cantwell Smith, *Occasional Papers* (Department of Missionary Studies, London) No. 5, April 1960.
11. *Young India*, 4-3-1926.
12. *Harijan*, 11-5-1935.

(iv) ISLAM

1. *Harijan*, 13-7-1940.
2. C. F. Andrews, *Mahatma Gandhi's Ideas*, p. 62, vide ante.
3. *Ibid.*, p. 62.
4. *Young India*, 10-7-1924.
5. *Ibid.*, 29-9-1921.
6. *Ibid.*, 10-7-1924.
7. Koran, XIV, V. 36.
8. *Ibid.*, XIV. V. 4.
9. *Ibid.*, II. 136.
10. *Ibid.*, XIII. 13.
11. *Young India*, 24-11-1921.

(v) THE PROBLEM OF HINDU-MUSLIM UNITY

1. *Young India*, 20-2-1930.
2. *Ibid.*, 27-1-1927.
3. *Ibid.*, 2-12-1920.
4. *Ibid.*, 25-9-1924.
5. *Ibid.*, 25-9-1924.
6. *Ibid.*, 25-2-1920.
7. T. W. Arnold, *The Preaching of Islam*, Sh. Muhammad Ashraf, 1961.
8. *Harijan*, 29-10-1938.
9. *Ibid.*, 15-12-1936.
10. Quoted in *The Philosophy of Mahatma Gandhi and Other Essays* by A. R. Wadia.
11. Jawaharlal Nehru, *Autobiography*, Allied Publishers, New Delhi, 1962.
12. *Young India*, 25-2-1920.

## Chapter 3

# PRINCIPLES OF CREATIVE RELIGION

### (i) Religious Experience

RELIGION has been one of the earliest, most constant, deepest, and most engrossing forms of human activity. It is a universal phenomenon in recorded human history. True religion arises out of life and is intimately connected with life. It is a continuous and constructive element in human development, and represents the eternal quest of humanity. It seeks to present a view of the world and a way of life which satisfy the spiritual and emotional needs of men and women.

Having its roots in the human mind and heart, it shows a marked tendency to perpetuate itself in one form or another. Religion is a process that has two sides, an inner and an outer. From the one point of view it is a state of belief and experience, an inward spiritual faith; from the other it is the expression of a faith in appropriate acts. Both aspects are essential to the nature of religion, and they act and react on one another throughout the process of spiritual growth.

At the back of religious experience is the fundamental fact that men and women are incomplete and imperfect, and their incompleteness or imperfection is revealed in a constant quest for a higher and a fuller life. It arises from their longing for the infinite Truth. What they seek from religion is the harmony and satisfaction for their inner nature, which they are unable to obtain by any other means or activity.

Religion is an upsurge from within. "Whenever a human being strives upward, toward enlightenment, goodness, and concern for others, the spirit of religion is active."[1] The secret of its strength and growth cannot be traced merely to the events of the outer world; they are to be traced to the realm of the spirit. Religious faith is thus an attitude and a state of mind. People have also other abiding needs, like hunger, love, self-expression, etc., which are ingrained in human nature. What is characteristic of them is their inescapable demand for satisfaction. Similar seems to be the religious urge. Religion represents a felt need, and this is the secret of its persistence. The deepest need of the human individual is religious. The animist as much as the monotheist responds to the same needs of his nature. "Man does not live by bread alone" (Deut. 8:3) expresses this truth in the Bible. "*na vittena tarpaṇīyo manuṣyaḥ*"[2] is the Upaniṣadic expression of the idea; it means : "Man does not find abiding satisfaction in the goods of the world."

Restlessness, lack of harmony, and the absence of a sense of direction in life constrain men and women to look for some source of strength and harmony within and beyond themselves. Religion is a permanent relationship between human beings and the universe in which they live. It has an element of the unknown in it which cannot be explained by grammar or logic. Count Leo Tolstoy observes, "A rational man has always been obliged in relation to the infinitely small phenomena of life which may influence his acts to make, and has always made, what in mathematics is called integration, that is, to establish besides his relation to the nearest phenomena of life, his relation to the whole universe, infinite in time and space, comprehending life as one whole. Such an establishment of man's relation to the whole, of which he feels himself to be a part and from which he deduces guidance in his actions, is what has been called religion. Therefore religion has always been and always must be a necessity and an irremovable condition of the life of a rational man and of rational humanity."[3]

Skeptics like David Hume have thought that fear is the motive of religious acts. Though there is this element in religion, it cannot be accepted as a sufficient explanation of religion. It can be even more clearly shown that love has played a more dominant part in religion than fear. Religion is something that is born out of the deepest instincts of humanity, and not imposed by the superstitious fear of the priest or the anger of God. A. E. Taylor thinks that religion originates in ancestor worship and is a primitive attempt to explain the phenomena of nature. Durkheim attempts to make "totemism", the matrix of all religion and society, as the real object of religious cult.

J. G. Frazer, author of *The Golden Bough*, holds that religion was adopted as a means of mastering life when magic did not deliver the goods. Sigmund Freud sees the origin of religion in an "Oedipus complex" in the primitive horde and in the projection of fears and wishful thinking.

According to Rudolf Otto, the origin of religion is neither a historical problem nor a psychological one nor a sociological one. The awareness of an unknown power or reality, the idea of something holy and sacred, is the essence of religion. "This mental state," he says, "is perfectly *sui generis* and irreducible to any other."[4] Religious consciousness points to something beyond humanity. Reverence for or worship of the unknown is the unique essence of religion, though this too is mingled with ethical and aesthetic categories.

In their origins the present world religions were simple; their prophets and seers spoke directly to the human soul. Some spiritual experience or other is the beginning of all the great religions. It is the fact of spiritual experience, not mere intellectual curiosity, that gives birth to a religion. Every *avatāra* came not to teach but to awaken. Hence the simplicity and directness of the utterances of the Upaniṣadic sages, of Christ, of the Buddha, of Muhammad, and so on. The consciousness of the Divine was communicated to their disciples not only in words, but even more by the atmosphere in which they lived, stirring them to recognition and response. Most religions owe their origin to the appearance of such a prophet or an *avatāra*. They give an important place to the seers, prophets, and *avatāras*. As Dr. Radhakrishnan observes, "All religions owe their inspiration to the personal insights of their prophet-founders."[5] Some religions posit their appearance from time to time. According to the *Bhagavadgītā*: "Whenever *dharma* declines and *adharma* gets the ascendency, O Bhārata, I create Myself to uphold *dharma* again and again."[6] This the *avatāras* do by embodying the very principles they teach.

Even though prophets make great contributions to religion, they are not themselves religion. Albert Einstein, for example, made great contributions to science but he himself is not science. Religion like language is coeval with humanity. Though the religious personalities show the way, the spiritual authority is ultimately the spirit of God within humanity. Religion does not mean some extraneous element forced upon the individual by someone else. It is the inseparable constituent of man's spiritual existence. It is an inner experience. Each must discover his religion for himself. He may draw from all the religious heritage of mankind, but finally he has to find his own way.

Religious consciousness involves feeling, willing, and thinking though these psychical elements are seldom present in equal degree. The whole meaning of life cannot be found in the exercise of only one of these functions: whether cognition or affection or volition, or devotion to a single value either of truth or beauty or goodness. One-sided stress on any one of these elements has given rise to different theories and sects of religion. Religious consciousness advances in time from an imperfect form to a more adequate form. But at any stage, it is at once a belief, a feeling, and a practical activity of the will.

All persons who are religious accept the transcendental origin of the universe and everything in it. They have faith in the spiritual foundation of reality, in a moral foundation of the world, and in the good life of man as essential elements of religious life. And they *feel* deeply about that in which they have faith. Emotion and faith are thus inextricably united together. According to Rudolf Otto, awe and reverence for the holy are very deeply written into the religious experience of all people. Hence personal warmth, love, and devotion are very important elements in religious experience. It also involves action, the doing and non-doing of certain things. Certain actions are condemned and certain others are commended. That means that religion calls for a particular pattern of action. Prayer and worship are enjoined by all religions. The religious life at its best demands the dedication of all the energies and capacities of the self to the service of God and man.

There runs through all religions the impulse to attain communion and fellowship with the Transcendent, which alone can satisfy the deeper needs of the soul. The supramundane object of faith is considered to be of supreme and ultimate value. But different thinkers emphasize different aspects of truth and experience. Though they are not for this reason mistaken or false, they are incomplete and sometimes insufficient.

According to Mathew Arnold religion is "morality touched

with emotion."[7] Gandhi wrote, "As soon as we lose the moral basis we cease to be religious. There is no such thing as religion overriding morality. Man, for instance, cannot be untruthful, cruel, or incontinent and claim to have God on his side."[8] The idea that to be religious is to be able to talk about God, and to proclaim who and what He is, is a superficial one. People may know a great deal about God or think they know, and may enter into long discussions and arguments about Him. But if their own lives and actions are not influenced by what they say, it is all empty talk. But to Gandhi, religion was the source of power and light by which the human person's "life is ruled and motivated." While religion deals with good and evil conduct, we cannot forget that it deals with more than standards of conduct. The German philosopher Schleiermacher says that the essence of religion is to be found in the feeling of utter dependence upon the infinite reality, that is to say, God. According to Gandhi, "True religion is not a narrow dogma. It is not external observance. It is faith in God, and living in the presence of God."[9] No doubt the religious person feels dependent on a divine power. But religion cannot be limited to the mere feeling of dependence. According to the Danish philosopher Harold Hoffding, "That which expresses the innermost tendency of all religions is the axiom of conservation of values."[10] In the words of Gandhi, "To me religion means Truth, and *ahiṁsā* is the necessary and indispensable means for its discovery."[11]

Immanuel Kant says, "Religion is (subjectively regarded) the organization of all duties as divine commands."[12] According to Gandhi, "The ultimate definition of religion may be said to be obedience to the Law of God. God and His Law are synonymous terms. Therefore God signifies an unchanging and living Law. No one has ever really found Him. But *avatāras* and prophets, by means of their *tapasya*, have shown that the will of God or moral Law is at the heart of the universe giving commands that everyone must obey."[13] Kant fails to give a place to the free, loving relation between human beings and the Supreme being. He is nearer to the heart of morality than to the essence of religion. According to Alfred North Whitehead, "Religion is what the individual does with his solitariness."[14] Here the stress is on the personal aspect of religion. But the social aspect of religion, its expression in social institutions and traditions, is equally important.

The American philosopher John Dewey drops the noun "religion" and uses the adjective "religious." He says that "Any activity pursued in behalf of an ideal and against obstacles and in spite of threats of personal loss because of conviction of its general and enduring value is religious in quality."[15] He adds, "It is that reconstruction of good which is indicated by ideal ends."[16] According to Whitehead, "Religion is the vision of something which stands beyond, behind and within the passing flux of immediate things; something which is real, and yet wanting to be realized; something which is a remote possibility, and yet the greatest of present facts; something that gives meaning to all present facts; something that gives meaning to all that passes, and yet eludes apprehension; something whose possession is the final good, and yet is beyond all reach; something which is the ultimate ideal, and the hopeless quest."[17] To Gandhi religion is fundamentally an attitude of reverence reacting to reality as Truth, in every fiber of which there breathes the meaning of life — a living presence that unites each to all, and in which everything lives and moves. It is an emotional realization of what thought discovers as Truth.

In the words of Count Leo Tolstoy, "Every religion is the establishment of man's relation to the infinite existence to which he feels himself related and from which he deduces his rules of action. And so, if a religion does not establish man's relation to the infinite, as for example in the case of idolatry and sorcery, it is not a religion but only a degeneration of it. If a religion, though establishing man's relation to God, establishes this by means of assertions which are contrary to reason and contemporary knowledge so that a man cannot believe in these assertions, this is again not religion but only semblance. If a religion does not bind up man's life with the infinite existence, this is again not religion. Nor is that a religion which demands a faith in a proposition from which no definite direction for man's activity results. True religion is man's relation to the infinite life about him, as established by him, a relation which is concordant with reason and human knowledge and binds his life up with this infinity and governs his acts."[18]

It is significant that the great masters of religion dwell much on the practical aspects of religion and little on the dogmas and creeds; these men of original spiritual insight and experience do not mistake traditional forms of religious expression for inward faith. According to Gandhi, "Custom is not religion. Custom may change, but religion will remain unaltered."[19] The mystics of different religions have in common a greater interest in the experience and practice of religion than in its doctrine. To them religion is more than a creed or an ideology and cannot be understood when detached from actual living. As Gandhi sees, "Language is a limitation of the Truth, which can only be represented by life."[20] Religious life is a life of love. The ultimate reality which responds to the prayers of saints and mystics all the world over is more than a rational concept. For such persons the significance of religion lies in the realm of emotional satisfaction. To them religion means awe and holiness before a God whom their intellect cannot reach, but who through a deeper insight know is there without a doubt. Religious knowledge is not abstract and general like conceptual knowledge; it is knowledge through being, a spiritual experience. On the basis of the reality of this experience, the saints and mystics assert the truth of religion.

The different religions trace their origins back to such creative, spiritual experience on the part of their respective founders. The loftiest teachers of mankind — Zoroaster, Christ, the Buddha, Krishṇa of the Gītā, and Muhammad were all mystics. There is a remarkable resemblance in the outpourings of their hearts — love and joy of communion with the Divine. This experience is one of peace and *ānanda* (bliss). It brings a permanent enrichment of the whole being. But the experience from its very nature is not fully communicable. Thus symbols and suggestions are used to hint at the unspeakable spiritual experience; the mystery behind is unfathomable. Every mystic comes to interpret his flaming experience of a higher consciousness in the theological terms of the religion to which he belongs and in which he is brought up. Later these teachings are developed by the followers into a body of doctrines and dogmas, and the communion of the initial circle creates definite forms of worship and begins to organize itself into a new pattern. In the words of Whitehead, "The dogmas of religion are the attempts to formulate in private terms the truth disclosed in the religious experience of mankind."[22]

After the transcendental experience, the mystic begins to adjust his life and character to the new light given to him. He often voluntarily imposes on himself hard disciplines to make himself fit for the new life. He cuts new channels in his mind and closes up the old. Even the formalities of religion are set aside. As Whitehead says, "The formula is secondary to its meaning; it is in a sense a literary device. The formula sinks in importance or is even abandoned; but its meaning remains fructifying in the world, finding new expression to suit new circumstances. The formula was not wrong, but was limited to its sphere of thought."[23] According to the Bhagavadgītā, the spiritually awakened transcend the words of scripture.[24] To them creeds and dogmas become in a sense irrelevant. "The written code kills but the Spirit gives life." (2 Cor. 3:6). How can the words of scripture satisfy them when what they seek is the reality behind all words and all thought ? In the words of Dr. Radhakrishnan, "Belief and conduct, rites and ceremonies, dogmas and authorities are subordinate to the art of conscious self-delivery and contact with the Divine."[25] A truly religious person feels that his own existence is a matter between himself and God. "The intolerant use of religious dogmas has practically destroyed their utility for a great if not greater part of the civilized world."[26]

There is a difference between communion with reality and opinion about it, between the fact of God-consciousness and belief in God. The nature of reality is one, but doctrines about it are many. Claims to the infallibility of truths based on revelations mediated through human minds are not compatible with religion as an ever-advancing spiritual quest. The greatest spiritual leaders do not seek to confine the infinite variety of the spirit in man within the framework of a rigid code or system. This is more the work of priests and followers, who have all too often distorted the teachings of the masters into rigid formulas. In the process of filtration through the minds of lesser men, the revelations of the original masters suffer. Our aim should therefore, be to catch something of the spirit of the masters themselves by studying their lives and attending closely to their words. Otherwise we may get lost in interpretations and commentaries. As Whitehead observes, "Religions commit suicide when they find their inspiration in their dogmas. The inspiration of religion lies in the history of religion. By this I mean it is to be found in the primary expressions of the intuitions of the finest type of religious lives. The sources of religious beliefs are always growing, though some supreme expressions may lie in the past. Record of these sources are not formulas. They elicit in us intuitive response which pierces beyond dogma."[27]

The human heart yearns for worship. Man cannot worship an abstraction. Hence he is driven to symbolize. Religious worship satisfies the longing of the heart through symbols: fire in Zoroastrianism, sacred images in Hinduism, the cross in Christianity, the Kaaba and the Koran in Islam, the Wheel of the Law in Buddhism, etc. The symbol is the means of expressing in concrete form the content of religious experience. The use of symbols is universal. It serves to a great extent as an integrating factor in creating religious fellowship. A symbol in its true sense is a finite expression of the infinite Truth; it is a necessary means to evoke and convey realities which cannot be expressed or communicated directly. In this perspective, symbols are not just what they are in themselves, but more importantly what they signify, what they are in relation to their ultimate and eternal source. According to Whitehead, "Religion must employ myth and symbol; though they are inadequate they are necessary. For whatever has objective validity is capable of practical expression in terms of abstract concepts, so that a coherent doctrine arises which elucidates the world beyond the locus of the origin of dogmas in question."[28] Gandhi wrote, "When the symbol is made into a fetish and an instrument of proving the superiority of one's religion over others, it is fit only to be discarded."[29]

Unfortunately, the symbol is very frequently confounded with the reality; and the popular mind seeks to exhaust the richness of reality in some arbitrary symbol of human creation. The eternal Transcendent is imagined and shaped by the mind of the worshipers temporarily, in the form of a symbol, as an aid to concentration and adoration; it is a symbol of truth, not truth itself. Therefore Whitehead says, "The dogmas, however true, are only bits of truth, expressed in terms which in some ways are over-assertive and in other ways lose the essence of truth." Accordingly, "though dogmas have their measure of truth which is unalterable, in their forms they are narrow, limitative, and alterable; in effect untrue when carried over beyond the proper scope of their utility."[30]

Religious faith must satisfy not only the hunger of the heart, but also the demands of the intellect. To develop the forces of his soul, one needs to use one's reason and to carry one's ability to question and test to the utmost. True religion integrates the various aspects of mental life into a whole. In the words of Gandhi, "Every formula of every religion has, in this age of reason, to submit to the acid test of reason and universal assent."[31] Religious belief cannot be unreasonable, though it may not be rationally proved: "Religion without the backing of reason and enlightenment is a worthless sentiment which is found to die of inanition. It is knowledge that ultimately gives salvation."[32] Faith and reason are therefore complementary and mutually imply one another. They condition each other. "Faith is the function of the heart. It must be enforced by reason. The two are not antagonistic as some think. The more intense one's faith the more it whets one's reason. When faith becomes blind, it dies."[33] Reason is allied to man's profound passion, the aspiration to attain God. If its wings are not clipped, reason will soar beyond itself and become creative. Gandhi asserts that reason is a necessary tool for discovering our limitations. "I reject any religious doctrine that does not appeal to reason and is in conflict with morality."[34] Further, "I have found that mere appeal to reason does not answer where prejudices are age-long and based upon supposed religious authority. Reason has to be strengthened by suffering, and suffering opens the eye of understanding."[35]

Gandhi often claimed to hear the voice of God. He was in that sense a mystic. He often spoke of the "Inner Voice," which prompted him to take one or another course of action. It gave him guidance, for instance, in his attempts to solve the Hindu-Muslim problem in critical situations. God's voice may sound feeble; it is not the result of sensory cognition. The spirit is ordinarily a still small voice; it is not even rational cognition. It is very different from the ordinary types of knowledge; for it is intuitive knowledge, the foundation of all moral norms and religious values. This "Inner Voice" has been stifled in modern times, and many people have lost faith in the possibility of such perceptiveness. But Gandhi recognized the limitations of reason. He knew that mere speculation cannot yield true knowledge: "There are subjects where reason cannot take us far and we have to accept things on faith. Faith then does not contradict reason but transcends it. Faith is a kind of sixth sense which works in cases which are without the purview of reason."[36]

To Gandhi true religion is renunciation in and for love. Such renunciation is an expansion of oneself through love. It is only by renouncing worldliness that we can hope to transform the world ; and it is only as we deny the lower self that we can hope to realize the higher self. In their unregenerate state, men and women live according to the "flesh" rather than the "spirit", centered in themselves rather than in God. Consequently, they must undergo a radical transformation before they can live as truly spiritual human beings. Only by renunciation and self-abnegation can every trace of the ego which stands in the way of our surrender to God be overcome.

In the words of Swami Vivekananda, "The aim [of religion] is to get rid of nature's control over us. That is the goal of all religions. Each soul is potentially divine. The goal is to manifest this divinity within by controlling nature, external and internal. Do this either by work (*karmayoga*), or worship (*bhaktiyoga*) or philosophy (*jñānayoga*) — by one or more or all of these — and be free. This is the whole of religion. Doctrines, or dogmas, or rituals, or books, or temples or forms are but secondary details." Again, "I accept all the religions that were in the past and worship with them all; I worship God with every one of them, in whatever form they worship Him. I shall go to the mosque of the Muslim; I shall enter the Christian church and kneel before the Crucifix; I shall enter the Buddhist temple, where I shall take refuge in Buddha and His Law. I shall go into the forest and sit down in meditation with the Hindu, who is trying to find the Light which enlightens the hearts of everyone. ... The Bible, the Vedas, the Koran, and all other sacred books are so many pages, and an infinite number of pages remain yet to be unfolded. I shall leave my heart open for all of them."[37]

## (ii) TRUTH AND NONVIOLENCE

Gandhi was firmly of the belief that the religions of the world, while they differ in other respects, unitedly proclaim that nothing endures in this world but the truth. He was once questioned : "If all religions are true, what do you do when there are conflicting counsels ?" Gandhi answered, I have no difficulty in hitting upon the truth, because I am guided by certain fundamental maxims. Truth is superior to everything and I reject what conflicts with it. Similarly, that which is in conflict with nonviolence should be rejected. And on matters which can be reasoned out, that which conflicts with reason also must be rejected."[1] Further, he maintained that by the employment of truth and nonviolence, it is possible to discover the underlying unity among all religions: "That master key is truth and nonviolence. When I unlock the chest of a religion with this master key, I do not find it difficult to discover its likeness with other religions."[2]

To Gandhi Truth was of paramount importance. He frequently quoted a favorite Sanskrit verse which said: "There is no higher religion than Truth," (*satyānnāsti paro dharmaḥ*). And the way to Truth is through nonviolence. He gave these religious principles a practical turn. He believed that the salvation of humanity depended on the practice of these principles. Truth is the ground of all existence and is also the goal of life. The whole universe is but the manifestation of that Truth and all beings are fragments thereof. Truth is the ultimate reality, the Supreme Spirit; it is called God by the theists. It may be difficult to define God; but "the definition of Truth is deposited in every human heart. Truth is that which you believe to be true at this moment, and that is your God. If a man worships this relative truth, he is sure to obtain the absolute Truth, i.e., God, in course of time."[3] Gandhi was aware that the same Truth manifested itself in different forms to different individuals due to the imperfections and limitations of man. He saw consistency in thought, word, and action as an attribute of those men who valued truth above everything. He tried to unify all elements of himself by orientation toward the search for Truth.

For Gandhi, both politics and morality were an extension

of the pursuit of Truth. He thought that Truth should penetrate and become manifest in every field of human action. His attitudes toward beauty and the arts illustrate this point: "I see and find beauty through truth. All truths, not merely true ideas, but truthful faces, truthful pictures, truthful songs, are highly beautiful. Whenever men begin to see beauty in Truth, then art will arise. There is no beauty apart from Truth. ... Jesus was to my mind a supreme artist because he saw and expressed Truth, and so was Muhammad. Because both of them strove first for Truth, therefore the grace of expression naturally came in. Yet neither Jesus nor Muhammad wrote on art. That is the Truth and beauty I crave for, live for, and would die for."[3a]

Gandhi looked upon Truth as *sat*, *cit*, and *ānanda*: "The word *satya* is derived from *sat* which means 'being.' And nothing is or exists in reality except Truth. That is why *sat* or Truth is perhaps the most important name of God. In fact, it is more correct to say that Truth is God, than to say that God is Truth. But as we cannot do without a ruler or general, names of God such as King of Kings or the Almighty, are and will remain more usually current. On deeper thinking, however, it will be realized that *sat* or *satya* is the only correct and fully significant name of God."

"And where there is Truth there is also knowledge, pure knowledge, where there is no Truth there can be no true knowledge. That is why the word *cit* or knowledge is associated with the name of God. And where there is true knowledge, there is always bliss (*ānanda*). Sorrow has no place there. And even as Truth is eternal, so is the bliss derived from it. Hence we know God as *Sat-Cit-Ānanda*, one who combines in himself Truth, knowledge, and bliss."

"Devotion to this Truth is the sole reason for our existence. All our activities should be centered in Truth. Truth should be the very breath of our lives. When once this stage in the pilgrim's progress is reached, all other rules of correct living will come without effort, and obedience to them will be instinctive. But without Truth it would be impossible to observe any principles or rules of life."[4]

All spiritual literature glorifies truthfulness as the most important cornerstone in the edifice of a perfect life. In the

Upaniṣads, it is said, "To Truth the path lies through truth." It is this attitude of seeking Truth rather than imposing or blindly accepting dogmas, an attitude of experiencing the truths taught by religious scriptures, rather than simply criticizing them, that guided Gandhi in his life. That is why he called his autobiography *The Story of My Experiments with Truth.* According to him, "Truth is like a vast tree which yields more and more fruit, the more you nurture it. The deeper the search in the mine of Truth, the richer the discovery of the gems buried there in the shape of opening for an ever greater variety of service."[5]

Gandhi never used to affirm dogmatically that what he said was the only truth. He never claimed to know truth in any absolute sense, and he repeatedly reminded others that humanity's inability to know the Truth in all its fullness required that he maintain an open approach in its pursuit. He would not impose truth as he knew it on others. In all humility he would say, "For me, this is Truth as I see it now." He would also act in accordance with it with the same attitude of mind. He maintained that only when a person is not beguiled by the evanescent objects of the senses can he or she see Truth. Also, one has to be free from preconceptions and prejudices; only then can one hope to attain Truth. It is this factor that made him take to the vow of *ahiṁsā*. He wrote, "In the march towards Truth, anger, selfishness, hatred, etc., naturally give way, for otherwise Truth would be impossible to attain. A man who is swayed by passions may have good enough intentions, may be truthful in word, but he will never find Truth. A successful search for Truth means complete deliverance from the dual throng such as love and hate, happiness and misery."[6] He also considered courage to be essential in the search for Truth, and regarded fear of anything as incompatible with the search.

Jawaharlal Nehru makes a significant statement which is very relevant at this point. "Truth as Ultimate Reality, if such there is, must be eternal, imperishable, unchanging. But that eternal, infinite, and unchanging Truth cannot be apprehended in its fullness by the finite mind of man, which can only grasp, at the utmost, some small aspect of it limited by time and space and by the state of development of that mind and the prevailing ideology of that period. As the mind develops and enlarges its scope, as ideas change and new symbols are used to express that Truth, new aspects of it come to light, though the core of it may yet be the same. And so, truth has ever to be taught and renewed, reshaped and developed, so that, as understood by man, it might keep in line with the growth of his thought and the development of human life. Only then does it become a living Truth for humanity, supplying the essential need for which it craves and offering guidance in the present and for the future."[7] Those who think that Truth is in their exclusive keeping and that their religion is the only approach to God see only one of many sides of the infinite picture. In the words of Gandhi, "We cannot reach absolute Truth while we are in this body. Each one of us sees Truth from his own angle of vision, and hence only in fragments. It is commonly said that though God appears to different individuals in different aspects, he is still One. The same may be said of Truth, which is God. There is bound to be difference of opinion among us, finite beings, about Truth, which is infinite, for our individual notions of Truth are likely to be tainted by errors. Therefore there should be no compulsion or violence on our part in making others accept what we regard as Truth. On the other hand we should leave others free and bind only ourselves by our convictions."[8]

Truth and nonviolence are inseparable: "*Ahiṁsā* is my God and Truth is my God. When I look for *Ahiṁsā*, Truth says, 'Find it through me.' When I look for Truth, *Ahiṁsā* says, 'Find it through me.'"[9] Gandhi lived a life of truth and nonviolence in a world riddled with evil and falsehood. He had to bear the hatred and calumny of those who could not purify their personal and social lives. And yet he loved them all. For nonviolence, to Gandhi, was neither negative nor passive. It was a dynamic concept. Indeed it involved, necessarily, active dissociation with all that stood in the way of love — greed, wealth, privilege, power, cruelty, corruption, and hypocrisy. Though nonviolence is as old as Buddhism and Jainism, it is Gandhi's genius that made it work in defense of truth on a scale unparalleled in the history of humanity. It was his firm belief that any injury even to the least of living beings was an offence against God and the Universal moral law.

Gandhi was a practical idealist. He knew that human

beings are caught in the conflagration of violence. "The saying 'life lives on life' has a deep meaning in it. Man cannot for a moment live without consciously or unconsciously committing outward *hiṁsā*, destruction of life. The very fact of his living — eating, drinking, moving about — necessarily involves some *hiṁsā*, be it ever so minute. A votary of *ahiṁsā*, therefore, is true to his faith if the spring of all his actions is compassion, if he shuns to the best of his ability the destruction of the tiniest creature, tries to save it, and thus incessantly strives to be free from the deadly coil of *hiṁsā*. He will be constantly growing in self-restraint and compassion, but he can never become entirely free from outward *hiṁsā*."[9]

All the prophets of the great religions are one in recognizing the supremacy of the *ahiṁsā*, or love, and in proclaiming that mankind can sustain itself and progress only on the basis of *ahiṁsā*. If God is in all and thus all-pervasive, then all must be saved and no injury should be caused to any living being. Saving a being from pain is as important a duty as causing happiness. If God is Truth, then nonviolence is the way to realize Him. In the words of Gandhi, "Prophets and *avatāras* have also taught the lesson of *ahiṁsā*, more or less. Not one of them has professed to teach *hiṁsā*. *Hiṁsā* does not need to be taught. Human beings as animals are violent but as spirit are nonviolent. Either they progress towards *ahiṁsā* or rush to their doom. That is why the prophets and *avatāras* have taught the lesson of truth, harmony, brotherhood, justice, etc. — all attributes of *ahiṁsā*."[10]

The highest spiritual goal, or perfection, can be attained only through nonviolence. Since perfection consists in realizing the spirit that is identical in all beings, and violence would involve a denial of this truth, the means to realize the goal of perfection is through nonviolence only. Nonviolence is an expression of Truth. The religious teachers of the world lay the greatest stress on the practice of this virtue. The Vedic command runs: "Do not injure any being." The Buddha taught: "Let a man overcome anger by love; let him overcome evil by good; let him overcome the greedy by liberality, the liar by truth." Jesus declared: "Love your enemies, do good to those who hate you, bless those who curse you, pray for those who abuse you." (Luke 6:27) An early Christian

Father said, "Violence is not the attribute of God." The prophet of Islam declared. "He who digs a pit for his brother man falls into it himself." In the words of Gandhi, "*Ahiṁsā* and truth are so intertwined that it is practically impossible to disentangle and separate them. They are like the two sides of a coin, or rather a smooth unstamped metallic disc. Who can say which is the obverse and which the reverse ? Nevertheless, *ahiṁsā* is the means; Truth is the end. Means, to be means, must always be within our reach, and so *ahiṁsā* is our supreme duty. If we take care of the means, we are bound to reach the end sooner or later."[11]

*Ahiṁsā* is compassion and self-sacrifice. It is inevitably fearlessness. It does not of course imply any bravado. It is meant to be the manifestation of a severely disciplined soul, disciplined in the spirit of righteousness. Gandhi advocated "nonviolence of the strong, who would disdain to kill but would gladly die for the vindication of Truth." He adds, "Nonviolence to be a potent force must begin with the mind. Nonviolence of the mere body without the cooperation of the mind is nonviolence of the weak or the cowardly, and has therefore no potency. If we bear malice and hatred in our bosoms and pretend not to retaliate, it must recoil upon us and lead to our destruction."[12]

Since man is essentially spirit and he has to use his body only as expressing the spirit, any conduct that makes him brutal is evil. In fact the salvation of mankind rests in the employment of truth and nonviolence. Gandhi demonstrated that they can be employed as weapons of active political and social ends. If God is the Creator of all, as the world religions teach, then "Love your enemies" (Matt. 5:44) is its necessary corollary. If then we ignore the obligation of neighbourliness and do not serve the people, all our prayer and worship are in vain. "Religion of nonviolence is not meant merely for the *rishis* and saints. It is for the common people as well. Nonviolence is the law of our species as violence is the law of the brute. and he knows no law but that of physical might. The dignity of man requires obedience to a higher law, to the strength of the spirit. ... Nonviolence in its dynamic condition means conscious suffering. It does not mean meek submission to the will of the evildoer, but it means the putting of one's whole soul against the will of the tyrant. Working under this law of our being, it is possible for a single individual to defy the whole might of an unjust empire to save his honor, his religion, and lay the foundation for that empire's fall or its regeneration."[13]

Gandhi objected to violence because it destroys truth. "When it appears to do good, the good is only temporary; the evil it does is permanent."[14] Nonviolence or love is the only standard by which true action and social justice can be measured. "The essence of true religious teaching is that one should serve and befriend all. I learnt this in my mother's lap. You may refuse to call me a Hindu. I know no defense except to quote a line from Iqbal's famous song : *Majhab nahinsikhātā āpas men bair rakhnā*, meaning, "Religion does not teach us to bear ill-will towards one another." It is easy enough to be friendly to one's friends. But to befriend the one who regards himself as your enemy is the quintessence of true religion. The other is mere business."[15] Gandhi thought if one truly followed the practice of not being violent with others in thought, word, and deed, he would not only attain Truth for himself, but also spread the knowledge of Truth to others. For nonviolence is not only the means to Truth, but also part of Truth.

### (iii) Concept And Reality of God

Immanuel Kant declares that the three fundamental subjects with which religion deals are God, freedom of will, and the immortality of the soul. And the greatest of these is God. Kant rejects the rational proofs for the existence of God in his *Critique of Pure Reason*, though in his *Critique of Practical Reason* he establishes it on moral grounds. As a matter of fact, the issue concerning God's existence is not purely an intellectual one made in the light of solely rational considerations. It is a practical question. The soul oppressed by the limitations of its material environment is driven to seek deliverance by an act of faith, and through faith it wins the God it seeks.

Gandhi, answering the question of a correspondent regarding belief in God, said, "There are certain things which are self-proved and certain which are not proved at all. The existence of God is like a geometrical axiom. It may be beyond our heart grasp. Intellectual attempts are more or less failures, as a rational explanation cannot give you the faith in a living God. For it is a thing beyond the grasp of reason. It transcends reason. There are numerous phenomena from which you can reason out the existence of God; but I shall not insult your intelligence by offering you rational explanations, and begin with a simple childlike faith in God. If I exist, God exists. With me it is a necessity of my being as it is with millions. They may not be able to talk about it, but from their lives you can see that it is a part of their lives. I am only asking you to restore the belief that is undermined. In order to do so, you have to unlearn a lot of literature that dazzles your intelligence and throws you off your feet. Start with the faith which is also a token of humility and an admission that we know nothing, that we are less than atoms in this universe. We are less than atoms, I say, because the atom obeys the laws of its being, whereas we in the insolence of our ignorance deny the law of nature. But I have no argument to address to those who have no faith."[1] In the words of Radhakrishnan, "The men of experience feel the presence of God and do not argue about it. The shoals and shallows of existence are submerged in a flood-tide of Joy."[2]

What most people mean when they use the word God is a supernatural, spiritual being who is holy and supremely powerful, and has a certain control over their destiny. They regard him perhaps also as the Creator, moral Lawgiver, and Judge, and believe that He is omnipresent as an indwelling presence. And those persons who express a strong revolt against belief in God have in mind some special notion of God, and it is *this* particular conception that they object to, some inadequate view which they were taught in childhood and which they quite naturally assume is *the* conception of God. For instance, when Darwin propounded the theory of evolution, many theologians were frightened, and they all shouted that Darwin had killed the Creator. And if it appeared to them that God had deserted His world, it is because they had a wrong concept of Him or were searching for Him in the wrong place. He is in us and with us. He is within us; but we pass Him by. According to Gandhi, "My firm belief is that He reveals Himself daily to every human being, but we shut our eyes to the 'still small voice.' We shut our eyes to the 'Pillar of Fire' in front of us. I realize his omnipresence."[3]

In the midst of the disintegration of our ordinary religious dogmas, a fresh formulation of the concept of God is needed in our age. He is within us and outside us. He can be best comprehended in ourselves. Ordinarily popular religions exalt God only to make Him inaccessible and inscrutable. There are various conceptions of God. Some devotees think of Him as possessing both divine forms and attributes. Others speak of Him as having no form but being endowed with qualities. Others again, while they take note of the personal, stress the impersonal, of which the former is regarded as a manifestation. But usually the devotees worship and pray to the Divine through a particular manifestation or form which serves as a prop for supporting their faith. In fact, it is immaterial how God is named; it is enough if He is conceived as the spirit of righteousness (*ṛta*) ruling the universe. Among all peoples, the God of the cosmic order begins to show of signs of an ethical nature with the awakening of the moral consciousness in man. The very uniformity of mystical experience proves this truth. The Christian attains Him through worship of Christ, the *Vaiṣṇava* through the worship of *Viṣṇu,* and the Muslim through the worship of Allah. But the ultimate object is one, however differently called.

Gandhi wrote, "There are innumerable definitions of God, because His manifestations are innumerable. They overwhelm me with wonder and awe and for a moment stun me. But I worship God as Truth only. ..."[4] Elsewhere he stated, "To me God is Truth and Love; God is Ethics and Morality; God is Fearlessness; God is the essence of light and Life and yet He is above and beyond all these. God is conscience, He is even in the atheism of the atheist. For in His boundless love, God permits the atheist to live. He is the searcher of hearts. He transcends speech and reason. He knows our hearts better than we do ourselves. He does not take us at our word, for He knows that we often do not mean it, some knowingly and others unknowingly. He is a personal God to those who need His personal presence. He is embodied to those who need His touch. He is the purest essence. He simply is to those who have faith. He is all things to all men. He is in us and yet above and beyond us. ... He metes out the same measure to us that we mete out to our neighbors — men and brutes. With

Him ignorance is no excuse. And with all He is ever forgiving for He always gives us a chance to repent. He is the greatest democrat the world knows, for He leaves us 'unfettered' to make our own choice between evil and good. He is the greatest tyrant ever known, for He often dashes the cup from our lips and under cover of free will leaves us a margin so wholly inadequate as to provide only mirth for Himself at our expense. Therefore it is that Hinduism calls it all His sport — *līlā* — or calls it an illusion — *Māyā*; we are not, He alone is. And, if we will be, we must eternally sing His praise and do His will. Let us dance to the tune of His *bansī* (flute) and all would be well."[5]

Mystics of all ages have felt and experienced God as Life and Love and Infinitude. To them, God is as real as the perception of the external world to others. At the basis of all religions is the direct experience of God or Truth. It is the consciousness of the Sacred, which is, as Rudolf Otto has convincingly shown, *mysterium tremendum et fascinans*. It is the visible presence of a higher reality which paradoxically attracts and repels, lifts up and throws back, fascinates and terrifies at the same time. This awareness of the Sacred is the common spiritual basis of all religions. God is that mysterious and unknown power, fearful yet friendly, which manifests itself in the productive power of nature, in life and in death. "He made the world and made us. He demands righteousness and justice; yet ultimately he has a kindly attitude toward man, responding to his prayers."[6]

Gandhi did not see God as a mere abstract idea. He was for him a living presence as well as an inner voice, as He has been to all the great saints and mystics of the world and to founders of religions. The majesty and mystery of God is as much true today as always. "There is an indefinable, mysterious power that pervades everything. I feel it though I do not see it. It is this Unseen Power which makes itself felt and yet defies all proof because it is so unlike all that I perceive through my senses."[7]

That there is one undivided and indivisible spirit, above and below, within as without, beginningless and endless, is basic to all religions. God is both the Law and the Law-giver. In Theravāda Buddhism, *Dhamma* or the Law itself is supreme.

The true God of religion transcends sensory experience and leaves all human conceptions of Him rolling in the dust. In the words of Gandhi, "I do dimly perceive that while everything around me is ever-changing, ever-dying, there is underlying all that change a living power that is changeless, that holds together, that creates, dissolves, and recreates. That informing power or spirit is God. And since nothing else I see merely through the senses can or will persist, He alone is."[8]

The great prophets who have been responsible for the moral uplift of mankind have pointed out that God is the most compassionate and benevolent and merciful one. He does not need sacrifices, human or animal. What He demands is that men shall be righteous, and the only offering that He will accept is a pure and contrite heart. This is the most precious teaching of all the prophets.

It is the subjective need for prayer and worship that gives rise to the need for personifying the ultimate truth as God. The idea that God is the Supreme Person is central to most theistic traditions. The human mind finds it hard to grasp an abstract concept and feels the need to personify. Hence the tendency of most of the religions to be centered on some personal deity. According to those who believe in a personal God, love is the law of Life; God is the common Creator of all beings and is Himself of the nature of love. Each devotee is free to choose his favorite form of God (*Iṣṭadevatā*) for purposes of personal devotion. But that does not mean that other conceptions of God are false. It is desirable that each should hold fast to his own conviction and advance spiritually. God with form is as true as God without form. "I do not forbid images in prayer," said Gandhi, "I only prefer the worship of the formless. This preference is perhaps improper. One thing suits one man, another thing suits another man, and no comparison can fairly be made between the two."[9]

The statement that God is a person is generally taken to mean that He is conscious intelligence and will, although not subject to the limitations of human personality. As a matter of fact, to say God is Creator is to affirm that He is the eternal source of the universe and the ultimate explanation of the fact that the universe and man exist at all. As we have seen, Gandhi preferred to define the Supreme Being as Truth. He considered Truth as the ground of all existence and as the goal of life. "I do not regard God as a person. Truth for me is God, and God's law and God are not different things or facts, in the sense that an earthly king and his law are different : God is the law itself. Therefore, it is impossible to conceive God as breaking law."[10]

The glory of God is present in every blade of grass and in every living soul. To worship God is at the same time to find the inner self and its meaning. Gandhi observes: "We may not be God, but we are of God even as a little drop of water is of the ocean. Imagine it torn away from the ocean and flung millions of miles away; it becomes helpless, torn from its surroundings, and cannot feel the might and majesty of the great ocean. But if someone could point out to it that it was of the ocean, its faith would revive, it would dance with joy and the whole might and majesty of the ocean would be reflected in it."[11]

Human conceptions of God are not and cannot be final. They grow and change. The meaning and value of existence are grounded in God and therefore transcend any formulation of them that may be achieved by any particular group. God cannot be contained in any person's or group's conception of Him. Faith can point to God but must never pretend to contain Him. According to Gandhi, though He is known by a thousand names, He is one and the same to all. "The Allah of Islam is the same as the God of Christians and *Īśvara* of the Hindus. Even as there are numerous names of God in Hinduism, there are many names of God in Islam. The names do not indicate individuality but attributes, and little man has tried in his humble way to describe the Mighty God by giving Him attributes, though indescribable and immeasurable. Living faith in this God means acceptance of the brotherhood of mankind. It also means equal respect to all religions."[12] Elsewhere, he wrote, "God is certainly one. He has no second. He is unfathomable, unknowable and unknown to the vast majority of mankind. He is everywhere. He sees without eyes and hears without ears. He is formless and indivisible. He is uncreate, has no father, mother, or child; and yet He allows Himself to be worshiped even as stock and stone, although He is none of these things. He is the most elusive.

He is the nearest to us if we would but know the fact. But He is farthest from us when we do not want to realize His omnipresence."[13]

The concept of God is not identical among all peoples, but varies with differences in time and place. The concept itself is evolving with the advance of the emotional, intellectual, and spiritual life of man. With the progress of knowledge, the God idea will come to mean the creativity and worthwhileness of life, not so much as actually realized, but as potential and ultimately realizable. Hence it is and must be the common possession of mankind. As Gandhi explains, "The Muslim says: He is and there is no one else. The Christian says the same thing, and so does the Hindu, and if I may say so, even the Buddhist says the same thing in different words. We may each of us put our own interpretation on the word "God" — God who embraces not only this tiny globe of ours, but millions and billions of such globes. How can we little crawling creatures, so utterly helpless as He has made us, how can we possibly measure His greatness, His boundless love, His infinite compassion, such that He allows man insolently to deny Him, wrangle about Him, and cut the throat of his fellow men? How can we measure the greatness of God who is 'so forgiving, so divine'? Thus, though we may utter the same words, they have not the same meaning for us all."[14]

### (iv) Universal Ethics

The moral law as understood by Gandhi is the eternal and immutable law governing the whole of life and of the universe. He treated all those who believed in the moral law as one human brotherhood. The root meaning of religion is "that which binds." The root meaning of its Sanskrit equivalent, *dharma*, is "that which holds." In Indian thought *dharma* means both religion and morality. *Dharma* sustains the individual as well as society. When morality incarnates itself in a living man it becomes religion. Gandhi once used to think of morality as the most important feature of religious life; but later on, he came to regard it as the very essence of religion. Experience taught him that the consciousness of moral values was something more universal and more definite than belief in God.

Religion in its historical manifestations represents the various ways in which the God idea has served as ground of the moral life. It relates the idea of God to the daily life of man. For the vast majority of mankind the need to lead a good life is far more imperative than anything else and that is why religions continue to have a deep significance for man. Gandhi met some people, in India and elsewhere, who upheld moral values but did not formally believe in God. Therefore he felt that the soul of practical religion was morality. "Mankind is one, seeing that all are equally subject to the moral law. All men are equal in God's eyes."[1]

In his autobiography, Gandhi wrote, "Morality is the basis of things, and Truth is the substance of morality."[2] Once morality was recognized as the fundamental factor in practical religion, it naturally followed that all religions were one in a fundamental way as they had the same basic moral principles. According to Gandhi, the task of religion has been to assert the supremacy of the moral law over the lives of men and nations. In the words of A. N. Whitehead, "What should emerge from religion is individual worth and character."[3]

Gandhi considered it necessary that men should intensify their moral and spiritual efforts for a deeper expression of their personality and creativity. And he thought if there should be a conflict between a religious doctrine and the moral imperative, the religious doctrine as formulated in the past must be expanded so as to include the moral truth incumbent on humanity. "If the morals of a man is a matter of no concern to him, the form of his worship in a particular manner, in a church, a mosque, or a temple, is an empty formula; it may even be a hindrance to individual or social growth, and insistence on a particular form or repetition of a credo may be a potent cause of violent quarrels leading to bloodshed and ending in utter disbelief in religion, i.e., God Himself."[4] A man's religion is to be judged not by his intellectual beliefs, but by his character and disposition. By their fruits and not by their beliefs do we know them.

Gandhi maintained that a human being is essentially a spiritual being. No one can be made moral or spiritual unless these qualities are native to and inherent in humanity. It is up to each person to realize his nature. So *sādhanā*, spiritual discipline, is necessary. The moral and the spiritual are fundamental elements to a meaningful life. Everyone who endeavors to act morally must also act on faith. For there is no way of knowing clearly what action in the end emerges as constructive or destructive, though there is an awareness that all actions should be done in response to God in consonance with His law.

The great prophets point out that God is not amoral or blind energy but a living Spirit, a moral will. He is righteous and demands goodness of His children. Religion is largely cultivation of the heart or ethical culture. The Buddha emphasized pure morality as the means to *Nirvāṇa*. Jesus Christ said, "Blessed are the pure in heart, for they shall see God." (Matt. 5:8) Gandhi wanted men to lead exemplary lives. He showed that moral codes of the various religions have striking similarities, and that all of them emphasize morality of a certain type. In fact, this was the origin of his idea of "ethical religion," which he presented in 1912 in a small booklet called *Neeti Dharma*. He held that there can be no correct ethics without an understanding of the foundations of ethical life in the recognition of the will of God. Each onward moral step in the history of religion has led to a deepening conception of God and that in its turn has strengthened the moral foundations of life. Gandhi wrote, in his *Ethical Religion*, "The general idea would seem to be that religion is something which is quite distinct from morality. In this book, however, no such distinction is recognized. Perhaps I shall be blamed for this by those who think that religion is not an element of morality, as well as by those who think that morality can dispense with religion altogether. Nevertheless, I venture to emphasize the vital connection between the two. ... Judging from the popular conception, it would seem as though religion were altogether independent of moral law. We come across many wicked men, priding themselves on their religiosity, while doing the most immoral deeds. On the other hand, there are also men, like the late Mr. Bradlaugh, who, while being extremely virtuous and moral, take pride in calling themselves atheists. Both these views are wrong."[5]

Moral conflict is rooted in the very nature of human evolution. All religions stress the moral struggle in the mind of man in the process of his realization of the good. It is not an easy struggle nor is it vain. Indeed, a single deviation from the path of rectitude on a person's part may create confusion and misery. Further, it is not easy to decide what is good and what is evil in a particular situation. Therefore, each person must shoulder the responsibility of solving every moral problem as it arises. For Gandhi, life was a process of self-purification, i.e., purging the heart of all impurities. He said, "It is the duty of every human being to look carefully within and see himself as he is, and spare no pains to improve himself in body, mind, and soul. He should realize the mischief wrought by injustice, wickedness, vanity, and the like and do his best to fight them."[6]

"Seek first his kingdom and his righteousness" (Matt. 6:33) is the call of Christianity and other great religions. His kingdom and his righteousness go hand in hand. Gandhi explained, "We find that the laws of conduct and morality laid down by the great religions of the world are practically the same. And all the greatest religious teachers have also proclaimed that religion is based on morality. Just as a building falls to the ground when the foundation is shaken, all religions must sink in the dust if their moral bases were to be disturbed."[7] In his autobiography, Gandhi wrote, "In my experiments everything relating to the soul has been a matter of morality; religion is morality. Morality from the standpoint of the soul is religion."[8]

Frequently, it is the creeds, liturgies, and fine theological points that have proved more attractive to a section of the followers of different religions than the moral precepts of the Masters and the spirit in which they lived. The thing most easily missed is the essence of any teaching. According to Gandhi, "Ours has become an age of hypocrisy and insincerity. Men, to whatever religion they may belong, care only for the external aspects of religion, and give the go-by to all its fundamental principles. In their lust for accumulation, they forget that they cause, or are likely to cause, harm to others."[9]

The moral life which may rightly be called religious implies belief in God and the immortality of the soul. Immanuel Kant thought that these beliefs were the postulates of moral life; for they encourage the pursuit of moral activities. In Gandhi's view, "A life of goodness is enjoined upon us, not because it will bring good to us, but because it is the eternal and immutable law of nature. Good works are indeed more than food and raiment to us. We should feel more grateful to one who gives us an opportunity of doing good deeds than to him who feeds us in hunger."[10] Such moral effort is essential and is not in vain as some persons consider it to be. If we understand by God a Power by whom the supreme values are maintained or achieved, the belief in such a Power would be an encouragement to us in our efforts. Religion at best directs and strengthens human response to the will of God. Only that person who is free from hatred and selfishness and who leads a life of purity and of disinterested service of his or her fellows can really be called religious or moral in the true sense of the term. As Gandhi has said, "Whatever the creed that a man professes, he cannot transgress the moral law except at his own peril."[11]

Moral life is fully concerned with one's relations to one's fellows; for instance, the injunction "You shall love your neighbor as yourself" (Matt. 22:35) implies the oneness of humanity and a sense of social responsibility. "A moral rule," according to Gandhi, "is a statement of a condition of social welfare and the highest moral law is that we should work unremittingly for the good of mankind." Loyalty to the Highest impels us to love our neighbors as well. Love of God and love of neighbor are the two sides, inward and outward, of a truly religious life. A good man is therefore not one who *can*, but one who *does*, act rightly. Virtue consists in the strenuous pursuit of the good irrespective of the consequence for oneself. In fact, spirituality without moral responsibility tends to become spurious. When we avoid the hard ethical demand that we love and serve our neighbor as ourselves, it is fatally easy to relapse into a superficial piety that makes no demand at all upon us but gives us personal consolation, peace, and security. Worship that seeks spiritual results for oneself without those results touching the lives of others is not the highest worship. The essence of genuine religion is the conviction that what we apprehend as the good for all ought to be actually made the supreme object of our endeavor. In that sense, it may be maintained that moral life ultimately depends on a religious conviction. That is, perhaps what Gandhi meant when he said, "No religion can exist without morality. Those men who follow morality for its own sake must really be regarded as religious."[12]

The morally good results from the effort to realize what is completely good in the wider sense of the term. Spiritual life stresses moral action of a certain type. It is not the morality of the customary or conventional type, which consists in one's conforming to the rules of conduct of one's society. At the spiritual level moral conduct springs from an acknowledgement by the individual of absolute moral value. It is not imposed upon the individual by his group or society without his consent. But organized religions, instead of allowing their followers to perceive and know for themselves what they ought to do, often dictate what they must do. They arise from sociological needs rather than from moral insight at the spiritual level. Mere conformity to social traditions is not morality in the highest sense of the term. In the opinion of Gandhi, "True morality consists not in following the beaten track, but in finding out the true path for ourselves and in fearlessly following it."[14] Further, "The great heroes of the world have always been those who went against convention or established precedent for the sake of doing good to the world."[14] This type of morality grows from within the individual conscience and becomes utterly imperative.

The growth of morality as a matter of conscience is largely the result of the interaction between the egoistic and the altruistic impulses. According to Gandhi, "The still small voice within must always be the final arbiter when there is a conflict of duty."[15] It demands obedience to unconditional or categorical imperatives and devotion to values regarded as finally valid. Morality of this kind is the primary form of spiritual activity, since it involves disinterested loyalty to absolute moral good; it involves an essentially religious attitude to moral law. The leaders of religion have been advocates of radical social change. They have been preachers of righteousness and heralds of justice. Socrates, the Buddha, Lao-tze, Jesus, Muhammad, and Gandhi were all of this type, pursuing the good in their own way, following their own moral insights, with great freedom blazing through ethical jungles. For them, "Spiritual obligation is of more consequence than social tradition."[16]

Immanuel Kant has told us that two things filled him with awe: "The starry heavens above and the moral law within." In his view the proper attitude of a person towards the moral law is one of 'respect.' Indeed, it is probably correct to say that most of those whose morality has been of this kind have been men of religious faith. In such men, morality is a part of religious life. Ethical thought, to be profound, must have a transcendental motive. Every human being is fundamentally a spirit, and in the depths of his being there is something that is immortal and absolutely real which gives meaning to his life. According to Gandhi, "The moral law has its seat in the soul of man. Truth is within ourselves. There is an inmost center in us all where Truth abides in fullness."[17] Further, he maintains, "No man can be called virtuous who is not fearless in the formation as well as expression of his opinion, and who does not unflinchingly obey the dictates of conscience. And this is impossible so long as he does not realize that the voice of conscience is the voice of God, and that it is the final judge of rightness or wrongness of every deed and every thought."[18]

To men of religion, power is of little significance compared to goodness, and goodness has gained a decisive victory over their desires. William James emphasizes the morality of God more than His power. J. S. Mill declared his willingness to go to hell rather than bend his knee to a powerful but unrighteous God. If God Himself is not righteous, His law cannot be morally binding simply because of His superior power.

Gandhi's emphasis on the moral law as a paramount principle of life holds out a great promise for a true renaissance of religion, freeing it from ritualism, dogmas, and doctrines, and releasing creativity of spirit. In his view, "the noblest of all aims is the worship of God. And the highest form of worship consists in doing the work of God by living in obedience to the moral law and by rendering disinterested service to humanity."[19] One meets one's God in the yearning of the human heart for goodness.

## (v) Prayer

Human beings express their feelings of dependence on God and their aspiration for the good, the true, and the beautiful by acts of prayer. Prayer posits man's awareness of a power in the universe greater than himself, which he cannot fully comprehend or measure. In all ages and religions, the spiritual aspirant and the devotee have given spontaneous expression to their innermost yearnings and deepest sentiments in hymns and prayers. They have sung and prayed from the fullness of their hearts. They have prayed not for the fulfillment of selfish desires but for the triumph of righteousness and to know the will of God in their lives. Prayer is both contemplation and adoration. It can arise from man's sense of need. With the consciousness of their limitations and helplessness men and women turn to the Omnipotent for solace and succor.

In the opinion of Gandhi, "Prayer is not asking. It is the longing of the soul. It is a daily admission of one's weakness. The tallest among us has a perpetual reminder of his nothingness before death, disease, old age, accidents, etc. We are living in the midst of death. What is the value of working for our schemes when they might be reduced to naught in the twinkling of an eye or when we may be equally swiftly and unawares taken away from them ? But we may feel strong as a rock if we can truthfully say, 'We work for God and His scheme.'"[1]

Prayer is the conversation of the devout soul with God. It puts the will of man in touch with the Divine Will. In moments of crisis, when life seems to go to pieces and the individual reaches an impasse, he instinctively reaches out to the higher power, who is regarded variously as Father, Mother, Master, Friend, Child, etc. Acts of worship and prayer prevent the trivialization of existence. They give the individual a sense of living in relationship with ultimate reality and teach man how to stand alone and yet not really alone. All religions indicate that prayer must be a matter of spiritual upliftment. It should mean the end of egotism and the beginning of a godly life lived in justice and peace.

To Gandhi, a life of prayer was a source of great comfort. He wrote, "Prayer has been the saving of my life. Without it, I should have been a lunatic long ago. My autobiography will tell you that I had my fair share of the bitterness of public and private experiences. They threw me into temporary despair, but if I was able to get rid of it, it was because of prayer. Now I may tell you that prayer has not been part of my life in the same sense that truth has been. It came out of sheer necessity, as I found myself in a plight when I could not possibly be happy without it. And the more my faith in God increased, the more irresistible the yearning for prayer. Life seemed to be dull and vacant without it. ... At that stage I felt as food was indispensable for the body, prayer was indispensable for the soul. In fact, food for the body is not so necessary as prayer for the soul. ... You cannot possibly have a surfeit of prayer. Three of the greatest teachers of the world, Buddha, Jesus, Muhammad, have left unimpeachable testimony that they found illumination through prayer and could not possibly live without it."[2]

What is of great worth in prayer is the contact of the finite individual's life with the infinite and the consciousness of the Infinite. Religion has the supreme function of kindling the human spirit by enabling it to make contact with the Divine through prayer. This conscious relation with God is a thing of great power and it brings an ever fuller spiritual growth and realization. It is an act of recollection by which man establishes and cultivates his communion with the source of all power. It is practiced by the Hindu, the Jew, the Christian, and the Muslim and even by the Australian aborigines and the Bantus in Africa. It is a spontaneous outcry of the mind. It lifts a man out of his immediate situation and makes him think about human life as a whole and about his existence in particular. It raises him above the everyday routine that threatens him with spiritual death. It reveals his potential power and leads to a harmonious and well-balanced life of happiness and peace. The form of prayer is not as important as the spirit, the will, and the aspiration behind it.

Regarding the time and duration of prayer, Gandhi wrote, "There can be no fixed rule laid down as to the time these devotional acts should take. It depends upon the individual temperament. These are precious moments in one's daily life. The exercises are intended to sober and humble us and enable us to realize that nothing happens without His will and that we are but 'clay in the hands of the Potter.' These are moments when one reviews one's immediate past, confesses one's weakness, asks for forgiveness and strength to be and do better. One minute may be enough for some, twenty-four hours may be too little for others. For those who are filled with the presence of God in their lives, to labor is to pray. The life is one continuous prayer or act of worship. For those others who act only to sin, to indulge themselves and live for self, no time is too much. If they had patience and faith and the will to be pure, they would pray till they felt the definite purifying presence of God within them. For us ordinary mortals, there must be a middle path between these extremes. ... Hence all religions set apart times for general devotion. Unfortunately, these have nowadays become merely mechanical and formal, where they are not hypocritical. What is necessary, therefore, is the correct attitude to accompany these devotions. ... Nothing can be grander than to ask God to make us just towards everything that lives."[3]

The real justification of prayer is to be found in the fact that it exerts a purifying influence on the mind and contributes to its development. Prayer helps concentration of the mind on higher things and thereby helps us attune ourselves to the spirit that illumines and elevates the world. Sincere prayers purify our hearts and make us better men. In the words of Gandhi, "Supplication, worship, prayer, are no superstitions; they are acts more real than the acts of eating, drinking, sitting, or walking. It is no exaggeration to say that they alone are real, all else is unreal. Such worship or prayer is no flight of eloquence; it is no lip-homage. It springs from the heart. If, therefore, we achieve that purity of heart when it is 'emptied of all but love,' if we keep all the chords in proper tune, they 'trembling pass in music out of sight.' Prayer needs no speech. It is itself independent of any sensuous effort. I have not the slightest doubt that prayer is an unfailing means of cleansing the heart of passions. But it must be combined with utmost humility."[4]

Prayer and worship have certainly an unquestioned place in spiritual life; they are indispensable for most devotees. The forces of good are strengthened by prayer. According to Gandhi, "There is an eternal struggle raging in man's breast between the powers of darkness and of light. And he who has not the sheet anchor of prayer to rely upon will be a victim to the powers of darkness. The man of prayer will be at peace with himself and with the whole world. The man who goes about the affairs of the world without a prayerful heart will be miserable and will make the world also miserable. Apart, therefore, from its bearing on man's condition after death, prayer has incalculable value for man in this world of the living. Prayer is the only means of bringing about orderliness and peace and repose in our daily acts."[5]

*Silent Prayer*

Gandhi used to retire for days together in times of crisis to talk it out with God, as it were. He had his silent prayers. In addition, he observed complete silence one full day in a week. In silent prayer an intensity of devotion can be achieved which in a dialogue with other human beings would scarcely be possible. Solitude adds a dimension, as it were; and the soul takes wings and soars. The splendor of God is beyond human words and thought. Its natural expression is often silence. All religions bear witness to this insight. The Bible calls it the "still small voice." The Koran says that Allah is a Power that works in silence. Silent prayer is a rich and liberating experience from which may spring forth many other uplifting activities. It may issue in thanksgiving, self-examination, penitence, or service. As a matter of fact, the value of prayer is only to be found when a person stands before God, without any reservation and in complete dedication in the fullest realization of his or her own littleness and of the immense power and love of God. That is fully possible only in silent prayer. And all religions recognize its importance and efficacy.

*Congregational Prayer*

Congregational prayer is practiced in and by all religions in some form or other. It involves a community of devout souls. Religion, whenever it is true to its highest purpose, tends to express itself in corporate and social forms. It is the genius of religion to create fellowship. Whenever religion is vital, it helps man in discovering value in others besides helping him to discover himself. It checks egotism and self-centered living; it breaks down barriers among human beings. No man is a whole of himself; his neighbors are the rest of him. It is said that where two or more persons gather in the name of God, there is the presence of God. Advising a student on this subject, Gandhi wrote, "A congregational prayer is a mighty thing. What we do not often do alone, we do together. ... Unconscious effect cannot be resisted. Are there not boys who at the commencement of their career were scoffers but who subsequently became mighty believers in the efficacy of congregational prayer ? It is a common experience for men who have no robust faith to seek the comfort of congregational prayer. All who flock to the churches, temples, or mosques are not scoffers or humbugs. They are often honest men and women. For them, congregational prayer is like a daily bath, a necessity of their existence. These places of worship are not a mere idle superstition to be swept away at the first opportunity. They have survived all attacks up to now and are likely to persist to the end of time."[6]

Further, congregational prayer raises the level of concern from the individual's own wants and needs to a concern for his or her fellows'. It gathers up the needs that are common to all humanity. It expresses a longing for social justice, brotherhood, and international peace. It is the best promoter of friendship and the best cure against unkind tempers and lower passions. The highest forms of prayer in all religions speak in the plural and voice the wish for the good of humanity as a whole. The Lord's Prayer reads :

Our Father who art in heaven
Hallowed be Thy name
Thy Kingdom come,
Thy will be done,
  On earth as it is in Heaven
Give us this day our daily bread;
And forgive us our debts,
  As we also have forgiven our debtors;
And lead us not into temptation,
  But deliver us from evil.[7]

The oft-repeated verses of the *Al Fatiha* when rendered into English read :

In the name of God, the most gracious,
  the most merciful,
Praise be to God,
The Cherisher and Sustainer of the worlds.

Most gracious and most merciful;
Ruler of the Day of Judgment,
Thee alone do we worship
And Thine alone do we seek.
Show us the straight way,
The way on whom Thou hast bestowed Thy grace
Not of those whose portion is wrath,
Nor of those who go astray.[8]

The Hindus worship the Supreme every day as follows :

May we meditate on the effulgent light of Him
Who is worshipful, and who has given birth
to all worlds.
May He direct the rays of our intelligence towards
The Path of Good.[9]

*Interreligious Prayer*

Cultivation of interreligious prayer is, according to Gandhi, desirable as an essential aspect of higher cultural and spiritual life. While everyone is free to follow his own religion as something good for himself, respect for religions other than his own is an essential requisite of cultural life and a fundamental necessity to the harmonious working of any decent society. To create a sense of unity, love, and respect for one another, it is useful that people should gather for interreligious prayers from time to time. The adherents of various religious faiths should be able to find a deeper unity of heart by worshiping God together. Community life may include morning and evening gatherings in common prayer and devotion, accompanied by sympathetic and respectful hearing of selected teachings of other religions.

In the common worship of the Supreme, the followers of different religions may join their hands and hearts; and stress should be laid on the universal aspect of the Divine, so that it may serve as a great bond uniting truly religious-minded people in different religions and inspire them to work together for the common good in a spirit of universal brotherhood. The prayers at Gandhi's *āshrams* in South Africa, and later in India, contained recitations from the scriptures of different religions.

His *āshram*, wherever it was, was a world in miniature. Followers of many religions saw the best of their own respective religions personified in Gandhi, and joined him in the type of prayer he advocated and practiced.

In "common prayer meetings," hymns that express the profound experience and vision of different religious teachers may be used. For example, Rabindranath Tagore's religious poems belong to this class. Tagore dispenses with the sectarian names and forms and makes use of the universal language of humanity. He speaks of God as Father, Friend, Master, Poet, King, etc., and his poems speak of the spiritual aspirations of the human heart. In the words of Horace Alexander, "For myself, I can say that I have known no experience so rich as the communion that comes of common worship with men of many faiths. In India, there is no difficulty in finding this experience. In some parts of the world, it is not easy. India can therefore contribute greatly to the harmony of mankind by showing how the harmony of the great faiths can be achieved. Let all who care for the heritage of Gandhi strive to develop that true tolerance which is based on reverence and friendship."[10] In common prayer, we do not think of ourselves. Our minds and hearts are turned to God and we strive to be attentive to His voice. This adds to the richness of the fellowship. Sincerity and humility enrich all. Gandhi often stressed that true prayer must lead us to action and towards selfless social service and justice in our dealings with others. There is no power so potent for right action as the power engendered by united prayer.

### *Āshram Prayers*

Gandhi rose punctually for morning and evening prayers, and his prayers were very regular. He found in his prayers a vital companionship with and an assurance of support from God. Though God is one, devotees worship Him through different names, forms, and ways according to their choice and temperament. In Gandhi's *āshrams*, whether in South Africa or in India, the principle of following one's own religion was adhered to; but, at the same time, all the members cultivated reverence for one another's religions. It was Gandhi's wish that, as every person took food according to his own taste and need, similarly in prayer everybody should get spiritual food according to his need and faith. Actually, whatever was read or sung in Gandhi's prayer meetings was neither sectarian nor in any sense narrow. Nothing delighted Gandhi more than to have readings and recitations from different religious scriptures. However the selections were spontaneous and reflected the religious trends and life in the *āshram.* Gandhi wrote, "In Phoenix [South Africa] we had our daily prayer. ... And Mussalmans as well as Christians attended them, along with Hindus. The late Sheth Rustomji and his children frequented the prayer meetings. Rustomji Sheth very much liked the Gujarati Bhajan *Mane Valum* : 'Dear, dear to me is the name of Rāma.' If my memory serves me right, Maganlal or Kashi was once leading us in singing this hymn, when Rustomji Sheth exclaimed joyously, 'Say the name of Hormazd instead of Rāma.' His suggestion was readily taken up, and after that whenever the Sheth was present, and sometimes even when he was not present, we put the name of Hormazd in place of Rāma. The late Hussain, son of Daud Sheth, often stayed at the Phoenix Āshram and enthusiastically joined our prayers. To the accompaniment of an organ, he used to sing in a very sweet voice the song *Hai Bahāre Bāg*: 'The garden of this world has only a momentary bloom.' He taught us all this song, which we also sang at prayers. Its inclusion in our *Bhajanāvalī* (prayerbook) is a tribute to truth-loving Hussain's memory. I have never met a young man who practices Truth more devotedly than Hussain. Joseph Royeppen often came to Phoenix. He was a Christian and his favourite hymn was '*Vaiṣṇava Janato*', he is a *Vaiṣṇava* (servant of the Lord) who succors people in distress. He loved music and once sang this hymn, saying 'Christian' in the place of '*Vaiṣṇava.*' The others accepted this reading with alacrity and I observed that this filled Joseph's heart with joy."[11] While Gandhi was living at Wardha, a Japanese Buddhist used to repeat some Buddhist *mantras.* When the war started, he was arrested by the government and was taken away. In memory of that pious Buddhist, Gandhi added that mantra to his āshram prayers. Miss Rehna Tyabji (daughter of Abbas Tyabji) arrived at Wardha to stay in Gandhi's āshram for a few days; she taught *Al Fatiha* and *Surat-E-Ikhlas* from the Koran to the members of the āshram. Thus verses of the Koran also made their way into the āshram prayers. In 1942, when Gandhi was interned at the Aga Khan Palace, Dr. Gilder was also confined there. Gandhi took this opportunity and invited him to join in prayers and requested him to help him with recitations from Zoroastrianism. Consequently, a Zoroastrian psalm became part of the āshram prayers.[12]

Once Gandhi asked Kaka Saheb, his learned disciple: "Today in the āshram, the majority are Hindus. If it were not like that and if Christians or Mussalmans were in majority, what would have been the form of our āshram prayers?" Kaka Saheb replied, "Just as we have taken verses from different religions, similarly we would have had selections from their prayers, too." Gandhi added, "Not merely that; we would have kept in the place of the Gītā, the Koran or the Bible. Our āshram is not of a single religion. It is of all religions. The environment should be conducive to all. This is the meaning of 'reverence for all *dharma*,' *sarva-dharma-sama-bhāva*."[13]

### (vi) Spiritual Growth and Salvation

All religions believe that the emancipation of the soul is the *summum bonum* of life; it is attained by grace and/or works as the fruition of the individual's search for God and selfless service of humanity. Salvation means literally being saved from death. Man is called *martya*, one who is liable to die. His desire, his hope, and his endeavor are that he may attain immortality. Of course, it is not physical immortality, but immortality of spirit. It means release from individuality and egoistic narrowness. According to Hinduism, the most important goal for each individual is to achieve freedom from past limitations and from the bondage of the wheel of birth and death by the realization of God within himself. Radhakrishnan observes, "In essence, religion is spiritual redemption and not social reform. Sanctity and holiness may imply service and fellowship, but cannot be equated with them."[1] Religious life is a new life; it is the God-guided life. It issues forth in the service of man. In the words of Gandhi, "Man's ultimate aim is the realization of God, and all his activities — social, religious — have to be guided by the ultimate aim of the vision of God. The immediate service of all human beings becomes a necessary part of the endeavor simply because the only way to God is to see Him in His creation and be one with it."[2]

Gandhi, as a *karmayogi*, gave his own interpretation to the doctrine of individual salvation. He distinguished between those who renounce the world to secure spiritual advancement in their quiet isolation and those who live in the world and fight the ills of humanity in a spirit of detachment. The latter consider life as an opportunity for salvation and worship, available only in this world, and therefore strive for those ideals as long as the body lasts. They are motivated by the desire to reduce the suffering of the teeming millions of the world. Gandhi conducted social experiments on a vast scale for the realization of Truth through love and service of humanity. Though most of these were carried in the political and social fields, he was prompted in all these things by his religious longing. He wrote "What I want to achieve, what I have been striving and pining to achieve these thirty years, is self-realization, to see God face to face, to attain *mokṣa.* I live and move and have my being in pursuit of this goal. All that I do by way of speaking and writing, and all my ventures in the political field are directed to this end."[3]

Gandhi belongs to that category of saints who live and work in society and yet whose only aim is religious emancipation. "My national service is part of my training for freeing my soul from the bondage of flesh — thus considered, my service may be regarded as purely selfish. I have no desire for the perishable kingdom of earth. I am striving for the Kingdom of Heaven, which is *mokṣa.* To attain my end, it is not necessary for me to seek the shelter of a cave. I carry one about me, if I would but know it. A cave-dweller can build castles in the air, whereas a dweller in a palace like Janaka has no castles to build. The cave-dweller who hovers round the world on the wings of thought has no peace. A Janaka, though living in the midst of 'pomp and circumstance,' may have the peace that 'passeth understanding.' For me, the road to salvation lies through an incessant toil in the service of my country and, through it, of humanity."[4]

The spiritual plane is linked with the ethical plane. Hindu thinkers call it *mokṣa*, which is the fulfillment of the highest values of life. According to Gandhi, "The aim of human life is *mokṣa*. As a Hindu, I believe that *mokṣa* is freedom from birth by breaking the bonds of flesh, by becoming one with God."[5] It is the God-conscious soul that attains spiritual repose in communion with Him and under the sacred shade of His overspreading love. In fact, spiritual experience is both the basis and the starting point of religion. Religious consciousness is the matrix of perpetual mental peace. It also produces a healthier human nature. The religious man has an equilibrium and spiritual stability that is proof against any disaster. Men must be underarched and supported from within. In the words of Gandhi, "*Mokṣa* is liberation from impure thought. Complete extinction of impure thought is impossible without ceaseless penance. There is only one way to achieve this. The moment an impure thought arises, confront it with a pure one. This is possible only with God's grace, and God's grace comes through ceaseless communion with Him and complete self-surrender."[6]

The chief purpose of all religious observances and spiritual practices is self-control and concentrated devotion to Truth (God). The desire for salvation provides the motive power for religious activity. Salvation is considered to be coming into the presence of God, which is possible from righteousness in thought and action. It is the realization of the unity of spirit transcending the limitations of space and time. It means more than a pious life; it is active participation in whatever plan or design God has for the whole of humanity and the world. William Law has written, "There is but one salvation for all mankind, and that is the life of God in the soul. ... That is God's gift to all Christians, Jews, and heathens. There is not one for the Jew, another for the Christian, and third for the heathen. No! God is one. Human nature is one. And there is the desire of the soul to God."[7] According to Gandhi, "No human being is so bad as to be beyond redemption; no human being is so perfect as to warrant his destroying him whom he wrongly considers to be wholly evil."[8]

The prophets of religions do not allow themselves to be overpowered by the sense of evil. All of them teach that evil can be overcome in the life of each individual, that *nirvāṇa* or *mokṣa* or the Kingdom of God is the right of everyone, and that when a soul purges itself of evil, and shines in the full glory of freedom from birth and death, then only the spirit in man becomes the ultimate victor. The prophets and saints of the world were all men of austere but noble and generous disposition. They shared their spiritual experiences with others for the elevation of humanity and taught the path to salvation.

Austerity, study, righteousness, society of the holy are aids to the spiritual unfoldment of men. Devotees with a strongly sectarian bias very often hold that salvation lies through the worship of a particular deity or incarnation and the acceptance of a particular religious tradition. But the truly religious lay aside the formalities of religion and take refuge in God. Actually, the important thing is to be saved from earthly bondage, and different religions help the respective followers to achieve this goal.

To Gandhi, the Kingdom of God is not a condition that waits in some undisclosed future; it is a present possibility of goodness hidden in every person. It is a condition of mind and soul which radiates peace, love, truth, and justice. He used to say, "I warn my Mussalman friends against misunderstanding me in my use of '*Rāmrāj*,' the Kingdom of God. For me Rām and Rahīm are one and the same deity. I acknowledge no other God but the God of Truth and Righteousness. Whether the Rāma of my imagination ever lived or not on this earth, the ancient ideal of *Rāmrāj* is undoubtedly one of true democracy in which the meanest citizen could be sure of swift justice."[9]

There are two apparently incompatible views regarding the initiative involved in the realization of *mokṣa.* One view says that salvation is entirely dependent on God, and man can do nothing but wait on His pleasure. If any particular person should be chosen, it is through the grace of God. The other view says that salvation is dependent on man's own effort. For instance, Southern Buddhism declares that man is required to find his *nirvāṇa* without external aid; man should free himself from evil and worldliness by his own exertion with discrimination. He should strive for *nirvāṇa* as long as his body lasts.

The incompatibility between the two views here is more apparent than real. Realization of the Kingdom of God is the meeting point of man's longing for God and God's descending to lift up man into His grace. Man's longing for God is itself due to His grace. So it is a continuous spiritual striving, at every point of which God's initiative and man's response are equally visible. The essence of salvation is illumination of the soul by divine grace, which involves a process of self-purification and self-realization. It is the spirit of devotion and comprehension that releases the latent spiritual powers in man.

**References**

(i) Religious Experience

1. *The Report of the University Education Commission*, 1948-49. (Govt. of India), Vol. I, p. 295.
2. *Kaṭhopanishad*, 1 : 27.
3. Leo Tolstoy, *Complete Works of Count Leo Tolstoy*, tr. & ed. Leo Wiener, Estes & Co., Boston, Vol. XXIV, p. 82.
4. Rudolf Otto, *The Idea of the Holy*, tr. J. W. Harvey, Oxford University Press, London, 1939.
5. Radhakrishnan, S., *An Idealist View of Life*, George Allen and Unwin Ltd., 1951. p. 89.
6. Bhagavadgītā, IV : 7.
7. Arnold Mathew, *Literature and Dogma*, The Macmillan Company, 1926, New York, p. 18.
8. *Young India*, 24-11-1921.
9. *Harijan*, 30-8-1938.
10. Hoffding Harold, *The Philosophy of Religion*, tr. B. E. Meyer, Macmillan & Co., 1906, p. 215.
11. *Young India*, 25-8-1920.
12. Immanuel, Kant, *Religion with the Limits of Reason Alone*, tr. Theodore Greene and Hoyt Hudson, The Open Court Publishing House, Chicago, 1934.
13. *Young India*, 25-8-1920.
14. A. N. Whitehead, *Religion in the Making*, The Macmillan Company, New York, 1926, p. 47.
15. John Dewey, *A Common Faith*, Yale University Press, New Haven, 1934, p. 27.
16. *Ibid.*, p. 27.
17. A. N. Whitehead, *Science and Modern World*, The Macmillan Company, New York, 1926, p. 191.
18. Leo Tolstoy, *op. cit.*, Vol. XXIV, p. 83-84.
19. *Young India*, 8-4-1926.
20. *Harijan*, 12-12-1936.
21. S. Radhakrishnan, *op. cit.*, p. 97.
22. A. N. Whitehead, *Religion in the Making*, p. 58.
23. *Ibid.*, p. 136.
24. See Bhagavadgītā, II. 46.

25. S. Radhakrishnan *Occasional Speeches and Writings*, Ministry of Information and Broadcasting, Delhi, 1960, p. 207.
26. A. N. Whitehead, *op. cit.*, p. 144.
27. *Ibid.*, p. 44.
28. *Ibid.*, p. 44.
29. Mahatma Gandhi, *An Autobiography*, vide ante, p. 480.
30. A. N. Whitehead, *op. cit.*, p. 145.
31. *Young India*, 20-2-1925.
32. *Ibid.*, 7-5-1925.
33. *Harijan*, 6-4-1940.
34. *Young India*, 21-7-1920.
35. *Ibid.*, 14-12-1928.
36. *Harijan*, 6-3-1937.
37. Swamy Nikhilananda (Ed.), *Vivekananda : The Yogas and Other Works*, R. V. Center, New York, 1953, p. 658 and p. 386.

### (ii) Truth and Nonviolence

1. *Harijan*, 6-3-1937.
2. *Ibid.*, 13-7-1940.
3. *Diary of Mahadev Desai*, tr. Ramanarayan Chaudhary, Akhil Bharat Sarva Seva Sangh, Kashi, 1961, Vol. I, p. 249.
3a. *Young India* 20-11-1924.
4. *Young India*, 30-7-1931.
5. M. K. Gandhi, *An Autobiography*, p. 268, vide ante.
6. *Ibid.*, p. 428.
7. Jawaharlal Nehru, *Autobiography*, p. 486, vide ante.
8. M. K. Gandhi, *op. cit.*, p. 6.
9. *Young India*, 4-6-1925.
10. M. K. Gandhi, *An Autobiography*, p. 348, vide ante.
11. *Harijan*, 11-8-1940.
12. M. K. Gandhi, *From Yervada Mandir*, tr. V. G. Desai, Navajivan, Ahmedabad, 1965, p. 13.
13. *Young India*, 2-4-1931.
14. *Ibid.*, 11-8-1920.
15. *Ibid.*, 21-5-1925.
16. *Harijan*, 11-5-1947.

### (iii) Concept and Reality of God

1. *Young India*, 24-9-1931.
2. *Religious Digest*, January-March, 1961.
3. *Young India*, 25-5-1921.
4. M. K. Gandhi, *An Autobiography*, p. 4, vide ante.
5. *Young India*, 5-3-1925.
6. G. T. W. Patrick, *Introduction to Philosophy*, Houghton Mifflin Co., Boston, 1924, p. 171.
7. *Young India*, 11-10-1928.
8. *Ibid.*, 11-10-1928.

9. *Diary of Mahadeva Desai*, Navajivan Publishing House, Ahmedabad, 1953, Vol. I, p. 168.
10. *Harijan*, 2-12-1939.
11. *Ibid.*, 3-6-1939.
12. *Ibid.*, 12-8-1938.
13. *Young India*, 25-9-1925.
14. *Ibid.*, 8-12-1927.

### (iv) Universal Ethics

1. M. K. Gandhi, *Ethical Religion*. tr. Rama Iyer, A. Ganeshan & Co., Madras, 1921, p. 47.
2. M. K. Gandhi, *An Autobiography*, p. 37, vide ante.
3. A. N. Whitehead, *Religion in the Making*, p. 17, vide ante.
4. *Harijan*, 30-1-1937.
5. Gandhi, M. K., *Ethical Religion*, p. 47, vide ante.
6. *Ibid.*, p. 35.
7. *Ibid.*, p. 48-49.
8. *An Autobiography*, p. 4, vide ante.
9. Gandhi, M. K., *Ethical Religion*, p. 61, vide ante.
10. *Ibid.*, p. 35.
11. *Ibid.*, p. 31.
12. *Ibid.*, p. 16.
13. *Ibid.*, p. 17.
14. *Ibid.*, p. 18.
15. *Young India*, 4-8-1920.
16. S. Radhakrishnan, *An Idealist View of Life*, p. 197, vide ante.
17. Gandhi, M. K., *Ethical Religion*, p. 44, vide ante.
18. *Ibid.*, p. 38.
19. *Ibid.*, p. 60.

### (v) Prayer

1. *Young India*, 21-9-1926.
2. *Ibid.*, 24-9-1931.
3. *Ibid.*, 10-6-1926.
4. M. K. Gandhi, *An Autobiography*, p. 96, vide ante.
5. *Young India*, 10-6-1926.
6. *Ibid.*, 23-9-1926.
7. Matthew, 6-9-13.
8. Koran.
9. Ṛgveda, III.62. 10.
10. Horace Alexander, in F. F. T. Quarterly.
11. *From Yervada Mandir*, Navajivan Publishing House, Ahmedabad, 1957, pp. 41-42.
12. See, *Ashram Bhajanavali* (in Hindi), Navjivan Publishing House, for the selection of prayers recited in Gandhi's āshram both mornings and evenings.
13. See, Introduction to *Ashram Bhajanavali* (in Hindi), Kaka Saheb Kalelkar.

### (vi) Spiritual Growth and Salvation

1. S. Radhakrishnan, *An Idealist View of Life*, p. 73, vide ante.
2. *Harijan*, 29-8-1936.
3. M. K. Gandhi, *An Autobiography*, p. xii, vide ante.
4. *Young India*, 3-4-1924.
5. *Ibid.*, 20-11-1924.
6. *Harijan*, 22-2-1942.
7. William Law, quoted in the *Report of the University Education Commission*, Government of India, Delhi, Vol. I, p. 296.
8. *Young India*, 26-3-1931.
9. *Ibid.*, 19-9-1929.

## CHAPTER 4

# INTER-RELIGIOUS RELATIONS

### (i) "REVERENCE FOR *dharma*"

GANDHI'S comparative study of religions led him to the appreciation of the best in every tradition and to the formulation of the concept of *sarva-dharma-samabhāva*; the expression implies looking on all religions with an equal eye. *Dharma* is what helps the evolution of the soul to a higher level of life; *adharma* is what obstructs its progress. Every religion, in essence, is *dharma*, since it aims to take human beings to a higher level of life. *Dharma* is derived from the Sanskrit root *dhṛ*, which means "to hold together"; it is the innermost constitution of a thing, the law of its inner being. It is an ethical concept which includes a moral code and the whole range of man's duties and responsibilities. This *dharma* is a part of *ṛta*, the fundamental moral law governing the whole universe, and humanity is to act in harmony with this moral order.

Gandhi maintained that one's religion is like one's own mother, entitled to one's highest reverence. He also accepted the moral and spiritual contents of all the great religions as equally valid for their respective followers. He accepted the religious experiences of the prophets of the world's religions as genuine. He saw no inconsistency in declaring that he "could, without in any way whatsoever impairing the dignity of Hinduism, pay equal respect to the best of Islam, Christianity, Zoroastrianism, and Judaism."[1] According to Gandhi, "reverence for *dharma*" expresses the ideal attitude towards the faiths of other men and their followers.

Different religious traditions do not admit of invidious comparisons since they emanate from different historical and cultural backgrounds. Hence, "reverence for *dharma*" does not mean that all religions are of equal value to all men; nor does it connote indifference to all of them; but it cherishes religiousness as expressed in each tradition. Just as all men are, in spite of their individual differences, equal before the law, so all the great religions are equal before God. He is concerned with every person, whether Hindu, Buddhist, Christian, Zoroastrian, or Muslim. Answering a question on this point, Gandhi once explained to Reverend Keithan, "All men are born equal and free, but one is much stronger or weaker than another physically and mentally. Therefore superficially there is no equality between the two. But there is an essential equality. In our nakedness, God is not going to think of me as Gandhi and you as Keithan. And what are we in this mighty universe? We are less than atoms, and as between atoms there is no use asking which is smaller and which is bigger; inherently we are equal. The differences of race and skin, of mind and body, and of climate and nature are transitory. In the same way, essentially all religions are equal. If you read the Bible, you must read it with the eye of a Christian, if you read the Gītā, you must read it with the eye of a Hindu. ... The tree of religion is the same, though there is not that physical equality between the branches. They are all growing, and the person who belongs to the growing branch must not gloat over it and say, 'Mine is the superior one.' None is superior and none is inferior to the other."[2] Just as one's own country is best for oneself, similarly each religion is very often adequate or the best for its respective adherents. There is one God who is working in the midst of all His people. We are all striving to know Him and His will. In that fundamental sense, all religions converge towards the same goal. Elsewhere Gandhi writes, "For me, all the principal religions are equal in the sense that they are all true. They are supplying a felt want in the spiritual progress of humanity."[3]

"Reverence for *dharma*" does not imply only co-existence with or toleration of other religions. Religious fanaticism of a virulent type may be slowly tending to disappear in the world. But that is not enough. Leaving other religions alone will not do; there should not be any tinge of malice or hypocrisy in one's attitude towards any other religion or its followers. According to Gandhi, tolerance "does not mean indifference towards one's own faith, but a more intelligent and purer love of it. Tolerance gives us spiritual insight, which is as far from fanaticism as the North Pole is from the South. True knowledge of religion breaks down the barriers between faith and faith.

Cultivation of tolerance for other faiths will impart to us a truer understanding of our own."[4] The term as Gandhi used it has nothing to do with mere "toleration." Gandhi gave a deeper and wider meaning to the word "tolerance." He drew it out of his *ahiṁsā*, nonviolence. His attitude was not only intellectually catholic, but also intensely passionate. The literal meaning of the word "tolerance" falls short of the significance he attached to it. It signified to him neither "sufference" nor "condescension"; but it sprang from his concern for truth. Tolerance should express a positive recognition of all the great religions of the world. In Sanskṛit, *samabhāva* means equal outlook. But in Gujarati, *samabhāva* means "sympathy." Gandhi evidently uses the word in the latter sense though the former is not excluded from it.* It encourages harmony and cooperation for common ends between the different religions. It is also a necessary social virtue. It implies unreserved freedom of thought and worship, and most of all it expresses a will to live in friendship with the whole wide world of humanity. Gandhi goes a step further : "I have, of course, always believed in the principle of religious tolerance. But I have even gone further. I have advanced from tolerance to equal respect of all religions."[5]

For Gandhi, toleration welcomed the enlightenment that may come from listening to a man with an alternative point of view. It implied a creative search for truth and value wherever it may be found. In one of his letters from the Yervada Central Prison, Gandhi wrote, "I do not like the word tolerance, but could not think of a better word. Tolerance may imply a gratuitous assumption of the inferiority of other faiths to one's own, whereas *ahiṁsā* teaches us to entertain the same respect for the religious faiths of others as we accord to our own, thus admitting the imperfection of the latter. This admission will be readily made by a seeker of Truth, who follows the law of Love. If we had attained the full vision of Truth, we would no longer be mere seekers, would have become one with God, for Truth is God. But being only seekers we prosecute our quest and are conscious of our imperfection. And

*This I write on the authority of Kaka Saheb Kalelkar, with whom Gandhi consulted when this phrase was coined in Yervada Central Prison.

if we are imperfect ourselves, religion as conceived by us must also be imperfect. We have not realized religion in its perfection, even as we have not realized God. Religion or our conception, being thus imperfect, is always subject to a process of evolution and reinterpretation. Progress towards Truth, towards God, is possible only because of such evolution. And if all faiths outlined by men are imperfect, the question of comparative merit does not arise. All faiths constitute a revelation of Truth, but all are imperfect and liable to error. Reverence for other faiths need not blind us to their faults. We must be keenly alive to the defects of our own faith also, yet not leave it on that account, but try to overcome those defects. Looking at all religions with an equal eye, we would not only not hesitate, but would think it our duty, to blend into our faith every acceptable feature of other faiths."

Gandhi continues : "The question then arises : why should there be so many different faiths ? The Soul is one, but the bodies which she animates are many. We cannot reduce the number of bodies : yet we recognize the untiy of the Soul. Even as a tree has a single trunk, but many branches and leaves, so is there one true and perfect Religion, but it becomes many as it passes through the human medium. The one Religion is beyond all speech. Imperfect men put in such language as they can command, and their words are interpreted by other men equally imperfect. Whose interpretation is to be held to be the right one ? Everybody is right from his own standpoint, but it is not impossible that everybody is wrong. Hence the necessity for tolerance. ... Tolerance obviously does not disturb the distinction between right and wrong, or good and evil. The reference here throughout is naturally to the principal faiths of the world. They are all based on common fundamentals. They have also produced great saints."[6]

Every religious tradition is orthodox to itself, though to some outsiders it may seem erroneous or heretical. There is no judge on earth who can judge between religions regarding the truth of their doctrines or the purity of their worship. A controversy that arises between religions over such matters is on both sides equal, and the only decision possible must come from the Supreme Judge of all men. Gandhi holds with modern Hinduism in general that "different religions express different facets of Truth; they are all true; but are tainted by the imperfect handling of imperfect men."[7] He pleads that no religion or religious group may judge another religion, lest it may be similarly judged; otherwise, unending charges and countercharges may ultimately lead to the denial of religion itself and consequently of the Godhead. "It is a travesty of true religion to consider one's own religion as superior and others' as inferior. All religions enjoin the worship of one God who is all-pervasive. He is present even in a droplet of water or in a tiny speck of dust. Even those who worship idols, worship not the stone of which it is made; they try to see God who resides in it. Various religions are like the leaves of a tree. No two leaves are alike, yet there is no antagonism between them or between the branches on which they grow. Even so there is an underlying unity in the variety which we see in God's creation."[8]

Gandhi maintained that a reverential study of the different religious traditions is a necessary part of a liberal education. "I hold that it is the duty of every cultured man and woman to read sympathetically the scriptures of the world. If we are to respect others' religions as we would have them to respect our own, a friendly study of the world's religions is a sacred duty. We need not dread, upon our grown-up children, the influences of scriptures other than our own. We liberalize their outlook upon life by encouraging them to study freely all that is clean. Fear there would be when someone reads his own scriptures to young people with the intention, secretly or openly, of converting them. He must then be biased in favor of his own scriptures. For myself, I regard my own study of and reverence for the Bible, the Koran, and other scriptures to be wholly consistent with my claim to be a staunch *sanātani* or orthodox Hindu. He is no *sanātani* Hindu who is narrow, bigoted, and considers evil to be good if it has the sanction of antiquity and is to be found supported in any Sanskrit book. I claim to be a staunch *sanātani* Hindu because, though I reject all that offends my moral sense, I find the Hindu scriptures satisfy the needs of the soul. My respectful study of other religions has not abated my reverence for or my faith in the Hindu scriptures. They have indeed left their deep mark on my understanding of the Hindu scriptures. They have broadened my view of life. They have enabled me to understand more clearly many an obscure passage in Hindu scriptures."[9]

"Reverence for *dharma*" is a consequence of the recognition of the spiritual values and insights embedded in every religion. It is an acknowledgement of the fact that different religions emphasize different facets of Truth, according to the genius of the respective peoples and the requirements of society. It is an expression of the belief that every religion is conducive to the spiritual advancement of its followers. It maintains that religions are not hostile to one another; it does not advocate displacement of any religion by any other religion. It rather persuades men to rise higher in the scale of spiritual development by following the true tenets of their own respective religious traditions and thus try to become better Hindus, Muslims, Christians, and so forth. One may, as a matter of fact, have preference for the particular framework within which one has chosen to live and act. Such a preference need not imply that one looks down upon all those who do not follow that particular framework.

Conscious reverence towards one's own religion and those of others is not possible unless one understands one's own religion at its highest and deepest and tries to understand other religions also in a similar way. As Gandhi observed, "In trying to explore the hidden treasures of ancient culture, I have come upon this inestimable boon, that all that is permanent in ancient Hindu culture is also to be found in the teachings of Jesus, Buddha, Muhammad, and Zoroaster."[10] Ignorance of one's own religion coupled with fanaticism often leads to perverse views about other religions. But he who understands and lives his religion in depth is truly filled with humble reverence to his own religion and similarly has the highest respect for every other religion.

To understand the point of view of a man of another faith requires broadmindedness, sympathy, humility, and willingness to recognize Truth, wherever it is. Only when equipped with these can a person appreciate alien traditions and conventions, beliefs, and ways of life. The prophets and seers of different religious traditions have brought mankind to a consciousness of the unity underlying the whole universe, a consciousness of the brotherhood of man and of the moral government of the world. These are some of the most important contributions of religious prophets to humanity, and none of them can be denied without loss to the spiritual worth of man. If the scriptures of others' traditions were to be read with mental reservations or ulterior motives, then the very purpose may be defeated and Truth may suffer.

Gandhi wrote, "When I was turning over the pages of the sacred books of different faiths for my own satisfaction, I became sufficiently familiar for my own purpose with Christianity, Islam, Zoroastrianism, Judaism, and Hinduism. In reading these texts, I can say I was equiminded towards all these faiths, although perhaps I was not then conscious of it. Refreshing memory of those days, I do not find I ever had the slightest desire to criticize any of these religions merely because they were not my own, but read each sacred book in a spirit of reverence and found the same fundamental morality in each. Some things I did not understand then, and do not understand even now, but experience has taught me that it is a mistake hastily to imagine that anything that we cannot understand is necessarily wrong. Some things which I did not understand first have since become as clear as daylight. Equimindedness helps us to solve many difficulties and even when we criticize anything, we express ourselves with a humility and courtesy which have no sting behind them."[11]

"Reverence for *dharma*" pleads that the task of reformation of religion must better be left to the followers of the religion concerned. Gandhi held that everyone should remain firm in his own faith and try to reform it from within; only then will their efforts be effective. However, he did not condone the lapses in his own religious tradition. He thought that by remaining a Hindu he could reform Hinduism better. He had realized that external criticism of the practices and popular beliefs of others' religions would not help. Destructive criticism from outside more often stiffened the practices and attitudes than remove them. His own mind in early life had revolted against Christianity because the Christian missionaries poured abuses on Hinduism. It had done more harm than good. It made it difficult for him to appreciate Christianity. Christian preachers stood in the way of his understanding Christianity. It is only after he came into contact with good and godly Christians and studied the New Testament that he could overcome the effects of the earlier distaste given by the missionaries. It was impossible for him to think that any religion could pull down or offend any other religion. He wrote, "No propaganda can be allowed which reviles other religions."[12] A person outside a particular religious group may point out the merits and excellences of another religion, may imbibe and assimilate into his own what is best in other religions, and may even offer helpful suggestions. But he may not condemn his neighbor's religion. For one thing, he has no right to do so. Only when one has befriended others does he earn the title to criticize. We must earn the title to criticize by showing reverence to the good elements in the faith of other men and by our friendly disposition towards them. The best that we can do is to seek understanding of another's faith or practice from the best interpreters of the religions concerned. The task of reformation should be left to the votaries of the religions themselves.

Pointing to some iniquitous injunctions and corruptions present in Islam, when a Muslim friend questioned Gandhi why he did not denounce them, Gandhi answered, "I have nowhere said that I believe literally in every word of the Koran, or, for the matter of that of any scripture in the world, but it is no business of mine to criticize the scriptures of other faiths or to point out their defects. It is and should be, however, my privilege to proclaim and practice the truths that there may be in them. I may not, therefore, criticize or condemn things in the Koran or the life of the Prophet that I cannot understand. But I welcome every opportunity to express my admiration for such aspects of his life as I have been able to appreciate and understand. As for things that present difficulties, I am content to see them through the eyes of devout Muslim friends, while I try to understand them with the help of writings of eminent Muslim expounders of Islam. It is only through such a reverential approach to faiths other than mine that I can realize the principle of equality of religions. But it is both my right and duty to point out the defects in Hinduism in order to purify it and keep it pure. But where non-Hindu critics set about criticizing Hinduism and cataloguing its faults, they blazon their own ignorance of Hinduism and their incapacity to regard it from the Hindu point of view. It distorts their vision and vitiates their judgment. Thus my own experience of the non-Hindu critics of Hinduism brings home to me my limitations and teaches me to be wary of launching on a criticism of Islam or Christianity and their founders."[13]

"Reverence for *dharma*" recognizes that all organized religions are aids and guides for the development and enrichment of the inner life of man. Religion is not an end-in-itself, but a means of attaining the highest moral and spiritual development. Different religions nourish, cherish, and provide every opportunity, guidance, and encouragement to the cultivation of the spiritual life by their respective followers. Mere outward conformity to the externals of an organized religion is not going to save any human being. It is the nobility and sublimity of the inner life of the great prophets of the world that command deep reverence, admiration, and emulation from human beings all over the world. Organized religions should nourish and cherish their respective spiritual aspirants and should join hands with one another in the promotion of spiritual life. "Reverence for *dharma*" maintains the possibility of such a spiritual fellowship of religions.

"Reverence for *dharma*" does not abolish the distinction between religion and irreligion. Gandhi observed, "We do not propose to cultivate toleration for irreligion. That being so, some people might object that there would be no room left for equimindedness if everyone took his own decision as to what was religion and what was irreligion. If we follow the Law of Love, we shall not bear any hatred towards the irreligious brother. On the contrary, we shall love him and therefore either we shall bring him to see the error or each will tolerate the other's difference of opinion. If the other party does not observe the Law of Love, he may be violent to us. If, however, we cherish real love for him, it will overcome his bitterness in the end. All obstacles in our path will vanish, if only we observe the golden rule that we must not be impertinent with those whom we may consider to be in error, but must be prepared, if need be, to suffer in our own person."[14]

Elsewhere Gandhi makes this point quite clear : "I should love all the men — not only in India but in the world — belonging to different faiths to become better people by contact with one another, and if that happens the world will be a much better place to live in than it is today. I plead for the broadest toleration and I am working to that end."[15]

## (ii) Evolution of the Concept

"Reverence for *dharma*" has run throughout Indian thought and culture since time immemorial, and Gandhi only embodied it more fully and clearly than before. India has been tolerant of alien faiths and has not hesitated to make friends with them. In the Ṛgveda, many centuries before the Christian era, we find it proclaimed: *ekam sat viprāḥ bahudhā vadanti*, ("Truth is one, and the sages call it by many names").[1] Very early in Indian history, the idea became popular with thinkers that the different names and forms of God do not, in fact, indicate difference. Differences in names and forms did not mean that the reality they stood for was not the same. This reverence for various forms of worship and systems of belief was animated by the conception that the Supreme Reality is ultimately One. Thus the conception of unity behind diversity has been a fundamental fact in the Indian religious consciousness from the very earliest times.

In Gauḍapāda's *Māṇḍūkya Kārikā*, it is said that Advaita Vedānta has no quarrel with anybody; there is a place for every religion and every school of philosophy in their respective spheres. It attempts to harmonize various doctrines and theories : *Parasparam virudhyante tenāyam na virudhyate*;[2] ("The other theories contradict one another, but this [i.e., *advaita*] is not contradicted by them." Similarly, in the *Pañcāyatana-pūja*, where *Śiva*, *Viṣṇu*, *Śakti*, *Sūrya*, and *Gaṇapati* are worshiped, there is the same breadth of vision and spirit of synthesis. So also *Brahmā*, *Viṣṇu*, and *Maheśvara* are synthesized and worshiped in the concept of *Trimūrti*, the three-fold form of God. One and the same *Īśvara* is viewed from different points of view, viz., creation, protection, and dissolution. Again, *Viṣṇu* and *Śiva* are worshiped in the symbol of *Harihara*; respect for the one depended on respect for the other as well. In Vedānta philosophy, *Advaita*, *Viśiṣṭādvaita*, and *Dvaita* are synthesized: "O Lord, while I identify myself with the body I am thy servant; when I consider myself as an individual soul, I am a part of Thee; and when I consider myself as the spirit, I am one with Thee — this is my firm conviction."[3]

Contemporary Hindu society also presents the spectacle of the different schools and sects of Hinduism living side by side in harmony. In fact, in India the same building and compound may house different deities and members of the same household would worship the different forms of God with profound reverence. Hindu tradition has generally represented this spirit of understanding and assimilation. And Gandhi was loyal to this spirit not merely in theory but in life. Hindu thought and culture flowered in him richly and authentically. He embodied this tradition fully and carried the same into new spheres of thought and activity.

Broadly speaking, Indian culture and religion have, from very early times, steered clear of fanaticism and exclusivism. The first message of peace and the power of love ever given to the world came out of India in the person of the Buddha. Face to face with human misery, in many forms, his great soul was tortured with pity and he cried out, "This is not the world for me. I wish to wipe every tear from every eye." Religious tolerance is depicted as a supreme virtue in Jaina scriptures. The term *sarvodaya*, as referring to all types of religious thought, is found in Jaina texts along with *anekāntavāda* (many points-of-view theory). The different schools of Buddhism and Jainism were looked upon as products of and included in Hinduism as they had many points in common with each other. Reverence for all religions has been not merely a matter of policy, but a fundamental principle of India's spiritual vision.

India has shown a remarkable spirit of accommodation to the followers of various religious traditions who sought shelter there, from time to time, to escape from being persecuted in their own homelands. After the second destruction of the Temple of Jerusalem, Jews came to India and were received here. They were given lands and homes and were allowed to live their own religion in their own way. Within a century of the death of Jesus Christ, the Syrian Church of Christianity could find a place and establish itself and carry on its activities freely in South India. And when Muslims invaded Persia, the remnants of the Zoroastrian community left their homes and came to India. They were well received and were provided with all the facilities to establish their own modes of religious worship. India met the Muslim traders with hospitality, and there were many happy contacts with Muslim countries long before the actual political invasions of Muslim rulers. As a matter of fact, when Christianity and Islam first came into India, there was no hostile resistance to them. It is rightly observed that "throughout the vicissitudes of India's history she tried to give expression to a sense of universality in religious as well as racial matters. Her outlook was ecumenical rather than parochial. She provided a home for each and every mode of universal tradition and did not exclude even those who had no faith in any religion."[4] We have also the very recent example of India offering shelter and hospitality to the Dalai Lama and his followers who came to India from Tibet.[5]

The *Bhagavadgītā* encourages freedom in religious matters and upholds a reverential attitude to various ways of life, thought systems, and spiritual disciplines. The following verses are typical of the attitude of toleration and understanding in the *Gītā* :

> Whatever form one desires to worship in faith and devotion, in that very form I make that faith of his secure. (VII.21)
>
> Even those who, devoted to other gods, worship them in full faith, even they, O Kaunteya, worship none but me, though not according to a recognized form. (IX.23)
>
> In whatever way men resort to Me, even so do I reward them. In every way, O Pārtha, the path men follow is Mine. (IV.23)

The *Śvetāśvatara Upaniṣad* says : "He who is one, and who dispenses the inherent needs of all peoples and all times, who is in the beginning and end of all things, may He unite us with the bond of Truth, of common fellowship, and of righteousness." (4:1)

The *Śivamahimna Stotra* proclaims : "Different are the paths laid down in the *Veda*, *Sāṅkhya*, *Yoga*, *Śaiva*, and *Vaiṣṇava* scriptures. Of these, some people take to one and some to another as the best. Devotees follow these diverse paths, straight or crooked, according to their different tendencies. Yet, O Lord,

Thou alone art the Ultimate Goal of all men, as is the ocean of all rivers."[6]

In the history of India, Aśoka's attitude towards all religions is typical of Indian culture and deserves special mention. In the very hour of triumph in battle, he gave up his imperialism to preach the gospel of peace and brotherhood and devoted the rest of his life to translating these ideals into action. His religious tolerance expressed itself as reverence for the religions of others. His famous "Rock-edicts" declare that everyone is free to choose his religion and worship in his own way. He constructed *vihāras*, monasteries, and presented them to *Jaina* ascetics, and made frequent offering of gifts and endowments to the followers of other religions. He was a Buddhist, but the ethical ideals of Buddhism have much in common with the best in Hinduism. In the enthronement of righteousness and true toleration, and above all of nonviolence, his endeavor is unique in history. His attitude to other religions was one of sympathetic understanding and reverence. He looked on the devout followers of all religions as fellow pilgrims, marching along the same arduous path of spiritual emancipation. The portrayal of this highest type of tolerance by Aśoka in Rock-edict XII finds no parallel elsewhere.

*Rock-Edict XII*

1. King Priyadarśin, beloved of the gods, reverences persons of all sects, and householders, by gifts and with various forms of reverence.
2. But the beloved of the gods does not value either gifts or reverential offerings so much as an increase of spiritual strength (*sāravṛddhi*) of the followers of all religions.
3. This increase of spiritual strength is of many forms.
4. But the root (*mūla*) is guarding of one's speech (*vacogupti*) so as to avoid the extolling of one's own religion and decrying of the religion of another or speaking of it without occasion or relevance.

5. As proper occasions arise, persons of other religions should be honored suitably. Acting in this manner, one certainly exalts one's own religion and also helps persons of other religions. Acting in a contrary manner, one injures one's own religion and also does disservice to the religion of others.
6. It is concord of all religions (*samavāya*) that is meritorious, as persons of other ways of thinking may thereby hear the *Dharma* and serve its cause.
7. This is the desire of *Devānāmpriya* beloved of gods, that the followers of all religions should be versed in many religions (*Bahuśruta*) and hold sound and righteous doctrines (*Kalyāṇa Āgama*), and in diverse places this should be stated by those present.

   Devānāmpriya does not value gifts and reverential offerings so much as an increase of spiritual strength of the followers of all religions.[7]

This philosophy of religious toleration as proclaimed by Aśoka in his inscriptions has spread from Peshavar in the North almost to Kanyākumāri in the South. Aśoka insisted on morality, simplicity, and truthfulness. Both the people and the King scrupulously practiced religious toleration.

Another remarkable instance of religious understanding is revealed in the *Śāsana* (royal edict) of the Keśava Temple at Belur, in South India. In the first verse of this *śāsana*, Śiva is praised along with Keśava. Another verse goes farther and prays that "Keśava, whom the Śaivas worship as Śiva, the Vedāntins as Brahman, the Buddhists as Buddha, the Naiyāyikas skilled in proof as Kartā, the followers of Jaina śāsana as *Arhat*, the Mīmāṁsakas as *karma*, and so on ... may fulfill our heart's desire."[8] Thus the devotee respects the different religious tenets as valuable and worthy.

Śrī Harsha (7th Century A.D.) was a Buddhist emperor who ruled throughout North India. But he was at the same time an admirer of other religions. His thinking was catholic and he paid respect to the learned men of all religions. He fed daily hundreds of Hindu and also Buddhist devotees. He built a number of monasteries and rest-houses for all religious people moving from place to place. Harsha received a religious delegation from China. It was during his time that the celebrated Chinese traveler Huein Tsang visited India. On his authority, we know that Śiva and Viṣṇu received equal honors with the Buddha. Harsha held an assembly of learned people of all religions, which was attended by Jains, Buddhists, Brahmins, and learned men of different schools of philosophy, and presented them all with innumerable gifts. Another Chinese traveler, Itsing tells us that the University of Nālandā was the meeting ground of the different sects and creeds with their "possible and impossible doctrines." Bāṇa's *Harsha-carita*, which belongs to the same period, refers to a meeting in Divākaramitra's hermitage of crowds of students belonging to different creeds : Hindu, Buddhist, Jain, and Lokāyata. "In Akbar's court there used to be friendly discussions among the followers of different religions."[9] Toynbee observes, "Akbar's Din-Ilahi was characteristically Indian in its large-hearted catholicity."[10] He tried to achieve a remarkable synthesis of Hinduism and Islam. Akbar represents the high watermark of Islam in India, in practice, as Aśoka did that of Buddhism. Their enlightenment and understanding has inspired men and women through history.

In the words of C. Rajagopalachari, "The tradition in Hinduism is that it is not open to any Hindu, whatever be the name and the mental image of the Supreme Being he uses for his devotional exercises, to deny the existence of the God that others worship. He can raise the name of his choice to that of the highest, but he cannot deny the divinity or the truth of the God of other denominations. The fervor of his own piety just gives predominance to the name and form he keeps for his own worship and contemplation, and he treats the other gods as deriving the divinity therefrom. This reduces all controversy to a devotional technique of concentration on a peculiar name and mental form or concrete symbol as representing the supreme being. It makes no difference in the contents of Vedānta to which all devotees equally subscribe. ... 'Just as all water raining from the skies goes to the ocean, worship of all gods goes to Keśava.' "[11]

"Even after the Muslim invasion of India," C. F. Andrews

observes, "immense efforts have been made by good people on both sides to overcome the profound incompatibilities that exist between Hinduism and Islam. In the Middle Ages, the great saints of Hinduism throughout the whole extent of North India made the most earnest and sustained effort to appreciate Islam. They interpreted the fundamental doctrine of the Unity of God as in accord with their own Upanishadic teaching. They even treated idolatry and caste as matters of supreme indifference. Furthermore, they paid respect to Islam along such lines of pure devotion and goodness that the Mussalman saints from their side — especially those who were called Sufis — welcomed Hindu religious philosophy and appreciated its ideals."[12]

Apart from the temporary tensions it created, the encounter of Hinduism and Islam has done lasting good to both religions. Prof. D. S. Sharma observes, "History has shown that both Hindus and Muslims had benefited by contact with one another. Muslims became less bigoted and Hindus became more single-minded in their devotions. And there arose teachers like Nanak, who said that he was neither a Hindu nor a Muslim, but a worshiper of the formless. He had come under the influences of both Hindu and Muslim teachers and was well-versed in the hymns of the Hindu saints and the writings of Sufi teachers. ... There was again Lord Caitanya, who had Muslim saints like Shaik Mohammed Sahib and Mohammed Kazi, as disciples, respected by both communities. And Kabir, who was a disciple of Rāmānanda, was very much influenced by Hinduism and Vedānta philosophy. He was also influenced by Sufi mystics who were Muslims. Though himself a Muslim weaver, his teaching shows the influence of Islam. "He [Kabir] accepts the Hindu doctrines of *karma* and *saṁsāra*, the Hindu concepts of *Brahman*, *māyā*, *lilā*, *mokṣa*, *vairāgya*, *sannyāsa*, and shares in the efficacy of the holy name *Rāma*. But he rejects the doctrine of *avatāras*, denounces idol worship and rituals. ... After his death he was claimed as a saint by both Hindus and Muslims. He was a real mystic to whom religion was a flaming personal experience."[13]

In earlier periods it seemed possible that a harmony between Hinduism and Islam could be attained. But crude orthodoxy on either side, leading to fanaticism and bigotry, stood in the way and has often thrown things back into conflict and confusion.

There have been many political upheavals in India. Kings have been deposed ; dynasties and empires have risen and fallen; political rivalries have resulted in division and revision of the boundaries of kingdoms. But so far as the cultural life of India is concerned, it has been one continuous flow. Max Müller observes, "There is, in fact, an unbroken continuity between the most modern and the most ancient phases of Hindu thought, extending more than 3,000 years." No doubt, it had to face many challenges in its course; and it reacted to them in a creative manner. During the course of its long history, it came into contact with a number of different peoples and cultures. It had to do with Greek, Iranian, Scythian, Hun, and Chinese, and ultimately with European, culture. In spite of all this it has been true to its roots and has not lost its identity. Its spirit has been "accommodative, adoptive, and assimilative rather than stiff and conservative."[14]

Political rulers and kings have generally respected the prevalent cultural and religious traditions and even appropriated the merits of the ideals and customs of the people over whom they established their sway. They gave generous endowments and gifts to different religious institutions. For example, the Chalukyas and Hoysalas defeated each other at different times; but they never interfered with the cultural and religious life of the people. On the contrary, they respected them by giving gifts of their own. The Pallava kings were regular patrons of Buddhism. Śaṁkara, the founder of the Advaita School of Vedānta, established his principal seat of learning at Śringeri with the help of the Vijayanagar kings. These endowments have been safeguarded by successive dynasties. Even the Muslim Nawabs continued these endowments. Nor was it unusual for kings of a different faith to patronize other faiths. As R. R. Diwakar observes, "It is a part of *rājadharma* (royal duty) to treat all religions equally."[15]

An important outcome of toleration and reverence towards religions other than one's own is the encouragement given to an impartial study and appreciation of other religions and the criticism of one's own in the light of different religions. Various religions, existing side by side, cannot but give rise to comparison of one with the other. Comparison is a halfway-house to constructive criticism; and constructive criticism results in religious reconstruction. There are always sensitive souls among the adherents of every religion who, keenly alive to the virtues of other religions and the shortcomings of their own, are stirred to reforming zeal. These reformers stress the need of inward faith and purity of thought rather than authority or book-learning or rituals. The Arya Samaj, the Brahma Samaj, and the Ramakrishna Mission are such movements of inner reform. The Theosophical movement, though born outside India, drew its main strength from India's ancient wisdom. Sri Ramakrishna is one of the most significant religious figures of the 19th century. His most important contribution is found in his insistence upon the validity of all the great religions. He entered into the spirit of the different religions by himself undergoing their respective disciplines of life. To Ramakrishna, the final test of truth is the experience of the Divine and therefore his attitude was experimental. Since all religions are valid paths to God, he thought, there was no point in leaving one for another. Indeed it is often best for a person to maintain allegiance to the religion in which he has been nurtured, which should not in any way preclude his taking new light from other religions and thus completing, as far as possible, his own religious *sādhanā*, or discipline.

2,500 years after the Buddha, we witness in India another great person who literally believed that violence and intolerance negated truth, that the greatest power on earth is the power of love in action, and that voluntary self-suffering can change the mind and heart of the most hostile persons. These are the teachings of Gandhi, who lifted the ancient and continuous tradition of tolerance and love in action to greater heights than ever before. Before Mahatma Gandhi there have been many teachers who have preached true reverence for others' faiths and put it into practice, too. But who else gave it such depth and width of meaning and who else exemplified it so fully in his own life as Gandhi? As Toynbee observes, "A spirit of nonviolence is a state of feeling inspired by a moral ideal. But every moral ideal is bound up with some corresponding intellectual outlook. And the Indian outlook, the intellectual counterpart of the Indian spirit of nonviolence, is a belief that, for us human beings, there is more than one approach to truth and to salvation. By 'truth' I mean a glimpse of absolute spiritual Reality. By 'salvation' I mean attaining harmony in some degree with Reality, when one has had a vision of Reality."[16] Elsewhere he writes, "And when the Mahatma and the Buddha speak with one voice, we are surely hearing the voice of India herself."[17]

Even today Hinduism is not the official religion of India. India is a land of many religions where adherents of all religions are on an equal footing. Gandhi wrote, "I do maintain that India's great faiths are all sufficing to her. Apart from Christianity and Judaism, Hinduism and its offshoots, and Islam, and Zoroastrianism are living faiths. No one faith is perfect. All faiths are equally dear to their respective votaries. What is wanted, therefore, is a living friendly contact among the followers of great religions of the world and not a clash among them in a fruitless attempt on the part of each community to show the superiority of its faith over the rest. Through such friendly contacts it will be possible for us all to rid our respective faiths of shortcomings and excrescences."[18] Hindus have therefore rightly refrained today from insisting that Hinduism be given a privileged status in India. In this, they have been true to India's own spirit and true to Gandhi who said, "I do not expect India of my dreams to develop one religion, i.e., to be wholly Hindu, or wholly Christian, or wholly Mussalman, but I want it to be wholly tolerant, with all its religions working side by side with one another."[19]

## (iii) Facets of Truth

Gandhi arrived at the concept of "reverence for *dharma*" in the course of his sincere search for Truth. He was conscious that his way of understanding Truth was not the only way. He had a great regard for the points of view of other persons. That was, for him, the practical meaning of charity. Because of his great concern for Truth, he was humble and inwardly receptive to other currents of Truth, coming from other sources. He never claimed finality for his won convictions. Otherwise he could never have said, "Truth is God." His concept of the harmony of religions and his reverence for all of them were the result of his ardent pursuit of Truth.

Feelings of superiority, exclusivism, mutual suspicion and

jealousy (latent or patent) are evident in the attitude of some of the adherents of religions in their relations with one another. The attitude which implies that one's own faith is the best and the highest and that other religious systems are imperfect or false produces a closed system. Fanaticism puts a stop to all religious quest and leads a person up a blind alley. It disables one from comprehending the growing fullness of Truth. So long as a person is unduly attached to certain preconceptions or prejudices one cannot hope to attain Truth. As one German philosopher observes, "The claim of exclusiveness is a moral attack on the search for Truth." Under these circumstances, "reverence for *dharma*" helps clear the air and produce harmony among various religions.

As we have seen, "reverence for *dharma*" *does not* postulate that all religions are of equal value to everyone and that a synthesis can be achieved by merely adding together the best in different religions. On the contrary, it maintains that they all have their own respective backgrounds and characteristics issuing forth from specific historical, geographical, and cultural circumstances. Persons with their specific backgrounds, the outcome of unique social and intellectual forces and often of an unrepeatable combination of historical factors, develop qualities which differ from those of others. It is that difference which expresses itself in the ethos of a people. The members of each religious group, too, share an outlook on the world, humanity, and God which is not identical with that of others. In the religious and cultural fields, there is a great scope for differences in methods of approach and modes of expression. It is therefore right and desirable to uphold the uniquenesses of particular religious systems. Cultural or creedal differences are not to be steamrollered; but attempts should be made to establish harmonious relationships between different cultures and creeds. This is to be achieved not in uniformity but in harmony. "Religious harmony is not attained when all religions surrender their historical individualities and hold a round-table conference of skeletons. Of course, when flesh and skin are removed from our bodies we are all one. But what we want is not unity in death, but unity in life."[1]

Gandhi *does not* look on eclecticism with favor. He does not approve of abdication of one's religion and its rich heritage.

On the contrary, he advocates firm adherence to one's own religion. The eclectic does not go deep into any religious tradition and therefore lacks depth; his approach is a superficial one and he fails to grasp the distinctive message of any religion. He swims on the surface only. "Well," says Gandhi, "to call a man eclectic is to say that he has no faith; but mine is a broad faith which does not oppose Christians — not even a Plymouth brother — not even the most fanatical Mussalman. It is a faith based on broadest possible toleration. I refuse to abuse a man for his fanatical deeds, because I try to see them from their point of view. It is that broad faith that sustains me."[2] Though Gandhi did not approve of an eclectic religion, he worked for a fellowship, a coming together of diverse faiths, each retaining its special fragrance, but entering into mutually respectful and fruitful intercourse with one another. Gandhi wrote, "I do not aim at fusion. Each religion has its own contribution to make to human evolution. I regard the great faiths of the world as so many branches of a tree, each distinct from the other though having the same source."[3]

"Reverence for *dharma*" requires individuals to keep their minds open towards other religions to understand and appreciate their spiritual and ethical contributions. It challenges them to listen to and to follow Truth wherever it may lead them. In the words of Gandhi, "The need of the moment is not one religion, but mutual respect and tolerance of devotees of the different religions. We want to reach not the dead level, but unity in diversity. Any attempt to root out traditions, effects of heredity, climate, and other surroundings not only is bound to fail, but is a sacrilege. The soul of religion is one but it is encased in a multitude of forms. The latter will persist to the end of time. Wise men will ignore the outward crust and see the same soul living under a variety of crusts."[4]

In the final analysis, every man must have a form of worship and set of beliefs suited to his own mental and moral competency. The food of the adult does not promote the infant's growth. We should leave everyone to his own mode of worship. All religions are relevant in the context of the diversity of human needs. "The roots of religion that lie in temperament are but poorly understood."[5] For instance, G. W. Allport points to the Hindu practice of receiving a suitable name of

God from a *guru* where "a young person with an unusually affectionate nature will seek in God the complement of his love. Hence the name 'Beloved' may be assigned to him. A theoretically minded youth may be advised to select '*So'ham,*' a name that affirms the unity of all existence."[6] Further, "The Hindu rite clearly recognizes underlying differences in temperamental constitution. Some men always live close to the region of pain and melancholy; they are bound to emphasize the grimmer aspects of whatever they encounter, and so stain their religious sentiment with their sense of forlornness. Others have started in life with sparklets of bells; even in their moments of despondence they incline to have a sanguine view of the operations of providence. Both the gloomy and the gay may be concerned with wrongness of life and may seek a religious mode of righting it, but their paths will be separate. Their theological and ritualistic preferences will differ according to their emotional thresholds, according to the quality of the prevailing mood, and according to their tendency to express or to inhibit feeling. Moreover, they are likely to be sharply biased in favor of these preferences, and correspondingly critical of others who find a different sort of religion better adapted to their needs."[7]

Some religions are strong in devotion (*bhakti*), some in knowledge (*jñāna*), and some in action (*karma*). Different types of men require different types of religious teaching. Though the fundamental truths of nearly all the great religions refer to the One God, they have to be presented to different people in different ways and in accordance with their temperaments and equipments (*adhikāra bheda*). In the words of Gandhi, "Belief in One God is the cornerstone of all religions. But I do not foresee a time when there would be only one religion on earth in practice. In theory, since there is One God, there can be only one religion. But in practice, no two persons I have known have had the same identical conception of God. Therefore there will perhaps always be different religions answering to different temperaments and climatic conditions."[8] This being so, there is no need to deplore the existence of various religions. All true values which enable and uplift life belong to God and must be respected and taken seriously. To ignore any of them is to ignore God's infinite richness and impoverish humanity spiritually.

The aim of all religions is spiritual salvation human beings. Different religions may appear in different stages of the quest for the Divine. They are all valuable, as each serves its respective adherents and lifts them higher. According to P. Sorokin, "The existing major religions, Christianity, Mohammedanism, Jainism, and others, do not need to be replaced by new religions or drastically modified. Their intuitive systems of reality value (God, Brahman, Tao, etc., as an infinite manifold) and their conception of man as an end value, as a son of God, as Divine soul, as bearer of the Absolute, these intuitions and conceptions are essentially valid and supremely edifying (in varying degrees for different religions). Similarly their ethical imperatives enjoining a union of man with the Absolute and the unconditional love of man for his fellows and for all living creatures call for no radical change. Some of these norms, such as those of the Sermon on the Mount, are indeed incapable of improvement."[9] The supreme need of today, therefore, is for a sympathetic understanding of the facets of Truth in different religious systems and their ways of life. Gandhi has said, "Religion is more than life. Remember that his own religion is the truest to every man even if it stands low in the scale of philosophical comparison."[10] Only by impartiality and charity can we recognize different viewpoints and work towards a greater harmony and cooperation than in the past. As a matter of fact, it is desirable that there should be differences between race and race, culture and culture, and that the human spirit should express itself in an infinite variety of ways, so long as they do not lead to conflicts and passions of hate and anger. As Dr. Radhakrishnan observes, "God wills a rich harmony, not a colorless uniformity."[11]

"Reverence for *dharma*" may be explained on the analogy of "freedom." Everyone should have freedom for the development of his or her personality. One should have freedom of speech, of movement, of worship, and so on. Freedom in all these spheres always means freedom consistent with a similar freedom for others. As Victor Hugo has put it, "the liberty of one individual ends where the liberty of another individual begins." Freedcm therefore is a social quality. It is also relative. If this freedom is to be ensured in the religious sphere, "reverence for *dharma*" is essential. As Gandhi reminds us, every religion has grown up in a particular environment; it has become associated with particular rituals and modes of worship. It may be necessary to preserve even the outward form as being the most suitable for the spiritual training of its followers. The great prophets propagated the truth looking to the conditions, the capacity, and the need of the recipients of the truth and the need of the times. Moreover, the religion to which a person belongs depends entirely on the society into which he happens to be born. He receives his morals and his religion from society ready-made. J. S. Mill observes, "It never troubles him that mere accident has decided which of these numerous [beliefs] is the object of his reliance, and the same causes which make a Christian in London would have made him a Buddhist or a Confucian in Pekin."[12] Everyone in every society should be free to follow the tenets of his or her own religion. And in freedom only can religion flourish; otherwise the situation becomes impossible. Let everyone be true to his or her faith, but not despise those of others. "The golden rule of conduct is mutual toleration seeing that we will never think all alike and we shall see Truth in fragments from different angles of vision. Conscience is not the same thing for all. Whilst, therefore, it is a good guide for individual conduct, imposition of that conduct on all will be an insufferable interference with everybody's freedom of conscience."[13]

The great religions of the world, each in its own sphere, have sustained the hearts and minds of millions of people down the ages. Each of them has an individuality, a message, and each has attempted to solve life's problems in its own way according to its own genius. All of them have supplied answers to the persisting questions of the mysteries of existence. They have lighted humanity on the path of right conduct and have given solace in the face of suffering and death. All deserve reverential study and understanding. In these days of materialism and skepticism, actually, the religions can fortify one another. If they fail to do so, religion itself may be in jeopardy. Unfortunately, sufficient attention has not been paid in this direction. If every religion aims at subverting other religions, then all religions will collectively perish giving rise to irreligion and materialism. Evidence of such a possibility is becoming increasingly obvious today. All religions should now cooperate to defeat such a calamity.

As Gandhi observed, "In nature there is a fundamental unity running through all the diversity we see about us. Religions are no exceptions to this natural law. They are given to mankind so as to accelerate the process of realization of fundamental unity."[14] The essential condition for progress in this direction is a frank acceptance by religious believers of the variety of religious experience and a willingness to recognize the truths in other religions. Genuine cooperation is possible only between those who respect one another. Religions often come into conflict with one another over trivialities — trivialities at least when compared to the spiritual truths in all religions which have moulded and are still moulding the lives of vast numbers of human beings. The universal principles of the Fatherhood of God and the Brotherhood of man, and of love as the fulfilling of the Divine Law, are without boundaries. Instead of putting our faith in these basic principles we sometimes stress trifling matters. This is a time for the greatness of religions to assert itself so that together the world religions can meet successfully the challenge of swiftly advancing materialism.

Apart from the broad groupings of mankind on the basis of religious affiliation, religion is also an individual attitude to life and reality and carries with it a sense of personal longing for the Divine. It is this element in religion that is perhaps expressed by A. N. Whitehead when he says that religion consists in what one does with his "solitariness." There are deeply religious men and women who are unable to derive help from any institutional religion as it exists presently. They find that they cannot accept the official interpretation of their scriptures. For example, among Christians or Hindus themselves, the theory of the world or the conception of the highest Reality, is not the same with each believer. In the words of G. W. Allport, "Most individuals are not sufficiently contemplative nor sufficiently imitative to adopt the explanation offered by any one master theologian. They may grasp parts of his system of thought and sense the direction of the system as a whole. But they find that they require their own interpretations when they are in the grip of engrossing troubles and turmoils of their lives. In times of acute distress, it is not the perfection of the system as a whole that satisfies, but some aspect of it that renders intelligible and supportable the needs of the moment."[15] Different individuals emphasize different aspects of the system. For them, therefore, religion is a thing of the heart and not merely of outward form. Hence every person should be entitled to his own conviction and, as a necessary corollary, should show respect for other's convictions.

Gandhi, as a man of action at the highest moral level, came to the concept of "reverence for *dharma*" through his own actual experience in nonviolence; it came to him as an inescapable corollary to nonviolent action. While in South Africa, he was engaged in fighting the government of South Africa with the weapon of *satyāgraha*, nonviolent resistance, because of the inhuman and unjust treatment to which it had subjected the Indian community. There were Hindus, Muslims, Christians, and Parsis in his nonviolent army. He could not have conducted the movement in a disciplined manner if he had differentiated among them on the basis of religion. The success of the *satyāgraha* struggle there was due primarily to the fact that the entire Indian community — Muslims, Hindus, Christians, etc. — stood solidly behind him and acted together as one. He realized, then, the practical importance and necessity of equal respect for all religions.

Dr. Radhakrishnan observes: "When two or three different systems claim that they contain the revelation of the very core and center of truth, and the acceptance of it is the exclusive pathway to Heaven, conflicts are inevitable. In such conflicts, one religion will not allow others to steal a march over it, and no one can gain ascendency until the world is reduced to dust and ashes. To obliterate every other religion than one's own is a sort of bolshevism in religion which we must try to prevent."[16] To fail here would lead to a state of anarchy in the moral and spiritual realm with repercussions in the social and political. Recent history in India bears ample testimony for this unhappy fact. In the words of Gandhi, "Mutual respect for one another's religion is inherent in a peaceful society. Free impact of ideas is impossible on any other condition. Religions are meant to tame our savage nature, not to let it loose. God is only one, though he has countless names. Don't you expect me to respect your faith ? If you do, may I not expect the same respect from you for mine ? ... The world is moving towards universal brotherhood when mankind will be one nation. Neither you nor I can stop the march towards our common destiny."[17]

All religions teach adherence to certain human and spiritual values, such as devotion to duty, righteousness, self-restraint, mercy, and, above all, devotion to truth and love. Every religion wants to disseminate these values in society. In this sense, the success of any religion is the success of all religions. In the eternal struggle of body and soul, religions have always taken sides with the soul and exhorted humanity to cultivate spiritual and moral values. Gandhi held that each religion must bring its individual contribution to humanity's understanding of the spiritual world. He readily welcomed the diversity of religious creeds by which men have sought to express their relation to the Supreme. "I believe that they are all God-given, and I believe that they were necessary for the people to whom these religions were revealed."[18]

Since the time the religious quest began, the horizon has continued to widen; prophets were born and are being born to give us different facets of Truth. God speaks to humanity at various times and in diverse tongues. Various persons, under different historical and geographical environments, are engaged in this eternal search for infinite Truth. A diversity of modes of thought and worship is not necessarily evil. The same Spirit informs them all. As we grow and progress in spirituality, we realize our kinship with one another through the universal spirit that binds us.

Truth in religion is understood in two ways : (i) it may mean that the doctrines of one's own religion are true and that everything else should be interpreted in terms of these doctrines. That is the theologian's position. True tolerance is impossible here. Such orthodox constructions militate against diversity of religions and contradict one another. (ii) Truth in religion may mean contact with or vision of Reality or God. This points to a commonly experienced Reality. Religious personalities have contact with the Divine. But one person's experience is not the only true experience. There is no case here for people to oppose religions other than their own. All religions are symbols and are all fulfilled in their own way by contact with the Supreme. "Reverence for *dharma*" understands Truth in this sense and advocates that each individual should start from his own religious foundation. But that does not mean that other ways to God are wrong. According to Gandhi, "When you consider other faiths as false, or so adulterated as to amount to falsity, you shut your eyes to the Truth that shines in other faiths and which gives equal peace and joy to their votaries."[19] Men and women must know that other ways to God exist that equally serve other people. The differing features which the religions display to the world are relative to the circumstances of time and place. It is not necessary to ask through which gate one enters the City of God. The important factor is the basic experience of the Divine, the living contact with God. In the absence of this, all forms and formalities are of little avail.

As we have noted, there are in the religions fundamental and eternal truths which give sustenance and inspiration to their followers. They supply some deep-felt inner need of human nature; the majority of mankind cannot do without them. But there are also accidental and surface elements. The task of separating the grain from the chaff is a difficult one. If this is accomplished, one sees the universal and lasting truths more clearly. In the words of Gandhi, "I would reject all authority if it is in conflict with sober reason or the dictates of the heart. Authority sustains and ennobles the weak when it is the handiwork of reason, but it degrades them when it supplants reason sanctified by the still small voice within."[20]

The spiritual truths contained in all religions are the common heritage of mankind. There is nothing like exclusive Eastern or Western spiritual values. Spiritual values are universal and cannot be confined to a geographical area or restricted to particular groups of people. Every human being has a right of access to these spiritual treasures. They are there to be studied, admired, and emulated; it is man's birthright. Reverence for all religions should therefore culminate in *mamabhāva*, i.e., the conscious acceptance of the entire human religious heritage as one's own. The prophets and saints of different religions have realized diverse spiritual truths after lifelong effort, struggle, and sacrifice, and passed them on for the benefit of humanity. These truths have a universal appeal. Anybody may draw inspiration from them. They are not the monopoly of any person or religion.

Most of the adherents of the great religions are hardly aware of the authentic content of their own respective traditions. They are satisfied, ordinarily, by adhering to certain rites and ceremonies. That is why mankind has never been kind to truly religious souls. Some of the prophets have died martyrs at the hands of their own people. What the world needs is the practice of true religion and not mere profession of it. The world has suffered not from lack of knowledge of morality, but from lack of right practice. The transformation can come only from self-purification and self-analysis.

Religions, in cooperation with one another, can do a great deal to rehabilitate mankind and give to life meaning, purpose, and value. They can also do much for the establishment of peace in the world. Where politicians have failed, religions may succeed, provided they cooperate and recognize their mutual worth and potentialities; and provided they pool together the tremendous resources of religions and channel them in the direction of world peace. The major world religions, in cooperation with one another, may bring out the latent treasures hidden in each religion and help humanity at a time when it is facing one of the most acute spiritual crisis in history.

The duty of all religions is to face up to the materialistic conception of the history of mankind. Human history is not animal history; it is not a mere fighting to satisfy hunger or to gain economic ends. It is the history of humanity's great spirits; it is essentially spiritual history. The followers of different religious traditions have to take note of the fact that, "all [religions] have saved a number of souls, but none has yet been able to spiritualize mankind. For that, what is needed is not a cult or creed, but a sustained and all-comprehending effort at spiritual self-evolution."[21] The great religions have to rise to the needs of the times and help to rehabilitate the human soul, which is being lost in sensuality and materialism. In short, "Man must come to realize that the tolerance with which Truth is pursued is not less important than Truth itself. If it be true that no divisions are so sharp as those caused by religion, it is equally true that no unity is so strong as that following a recognition of identity in religious aim, which is the supreme aim in life."[22]

**References**


(i) REVERENCE FOR DHARMA

1. *Harijan*, 30-11-1947.
2. *Harijan*, 13-3-1937.
3. *Harijan*, 6-4-1939.
4. *From Yervada Mandir*, tr. V. G. Desai, Navajivan Publishing House, Ahmedabad, 1957. p. 40.
5. *Harijan*, 12-1-1947.
6. M. K. Gandhi : *From Yervada Mandir*, op. cit., pp. 38-40.
7. *Young India*, 20-2-1930.
8. *Harijan*, 26-5-1946.
9. *Young India*, 2-9-1926.
10. Mahadev Desai, *With Gandhiji in Ceylon*, S. Ganeshan, Madras, 1928, p. 131.
11. *From Yervada Mandir*, pp. 42-43, vide ante.
12. *Young India*, 29-5-1924.
13. *Harijan*, 13-3-1937.
14. M. K. Gandhi : *From Yervada Mandir*, op. cit., pp. 43-44.
15. *Young India*, 22-12-1927.

(ii) EVOLUTION OF THE CONCEPT

1. Rigveda. 1: 164: 46.
2. *Māṇḍūkya Kārikā*, III, 17.
3. *Dehabuddhyā tu dāso'smi jīvabuddhyā tvadaṁśakaḥ,*
   *Ātmabuddhyā tvamevāham iti me niścitā matiḥ.*
4. *The Report of the University Education Commission*, Vol. I, p. 298, vide ante.
5. Asylum was provided by the Government of India to the Dalai Lama and Tibetan Refugees in 1959.
6. *Trayī sāṅkhyam yogaḥ paśupatimatam vaiṣṇavamiti prabhinne.*
7. *Edicts of Asoka*, trans. by G. Srinivasa Murthy and A. N. Krishna Iyengar, pp. 33-34.
8. *Yam śaivāḥ samupāsate śiva iti brahmeti vedāntino.*
9. Quoted in *The Report of the University Education Commission*, Vol. 1, Government of India Publications, New Delhi.
10. Arnold Toynbee, *One World and India*, Indian Council for Cultural Relations, New Delhi, p. 19.
11. C. Rajagopalachari, *Hinduism : Doctrine and Way of Life*, Bharatiya Vidya Bhavan, Bombay, 1970.
12. C. F. Andrews, *Mahatma Gandhi's Ideas*, p. 55, vide ante.
13. D. S. Sharma, *Hinduism Through the Ages*, Bharatiya Vidya Bhavan, Bombay, 1973, p. 90.

14. R. R. Diwakar, *Paramahamsa Ramakrishna*, Bharatiya Vidya Bhavan, Bombay, 1964. p. 31.
15. *Ibid.*, p. 30.
16. Arnold Toynbee, *One World and India*, p. 55, vide ante.
17. *Ibid.*, p. 50.
18. *Young India*, 23-4-1931.
19. *Ibid.*, 22-12-1927.

### (iii) Facets of Truth

1. D. S. Sharma, *Hinduism Through the Ages*, p. 76, vide ante.
2. *Young India*, 22-12-1927.
3. *Harijan*, 28-1-1938.
4. *Young India*, 25-9-1925.
5. G. W. Allport, *The Individual and His Religion*, Macmillan, New York, 1960, p. 12
6. *Ibid.*, p. 11.
7. *Ibid.*, p. 12.
8. R. K. Prabhu (ed.), *The Mind of Mahatma Gandhi*, p. 84.
9. Sorokin Pitirim., *Reconstruction of Humanity*, Beacon Press, Boston, 1948, p. 115.
10. *Young India*, 28-8-1924.
11. S. Radhakrishnan, *The Hindu View of Life*, p. 59, vide ante.
12. J. S. Mill, "Essay on Liberty."
13. *Young India*, 23-9-1926.
14. *Ibid.*, 20-8-1925.
15. Allport, G. W., *The Individual and His Religion*, p. 17, vide ante.
16. S. Radhakrishnan, *The Hindu View of Life*, p. 58, vide ante.
17. *Harijan*, 10-2-1940.
18. *Ibid.*, 16-2-1934.
19. *Ibid.*, 13-1-1940.
20. *Young India*, 18-12-1920.
21. Sri Aurobindo, *Thoughts and Glimpses*, Arya Publishing House, Calcutta, 1944, p. 40.
22. M. Hiriyanna, *Mission of Philosophy*, p. 45.

CHAPTER 5

# SOME COMMON PROBLEMS

## (i) THE PROBLEM OF CONVERSION

IN different ages, climes, and places humanity has striven to satisfy the hunger for God and has discovered various indigenous ways of satisfying it. The spiritual path to the ultimate found in a particular cultural, psychological, and social environment affords the best medium for those in that circle. Consequently no single religion is satisfying to all peoples. Historically, despite claims to the contrary, no religion has achieved perfection, and all traditions need the help of such ingredients from the others to make them richer, fuller, and more satisfying. The satisfaction of the spiritual hunger of a people, however, comes chiefly through their own religious tradition. All the principal religions have in them what can take a man to his highest goal. It is therefore not necessary for the spiritual emancipation of, say, a Christian or a Mussalman to make him a formal convert to Hinduism or Buddhism, or vice versa, especially because any man in any religion can freely draw from the heritage of other religions to add to his own.

In the opinion of Gandhi, all people should be firmly rooted in their respective traditions and then purify them if and where necessary. He was emphatically against proselytization. He wrote, "Religion is a matter of life and death. A man does not change his religion as he changes his garments. He takes it with him beyond the grave. Nor does a man profess his religion to oblige others. He professes a religion because he cannot do otherwise."[1] Gandhi believed that all religions are branches of one and the same tree — the tree of Truth. The shape and size of the branches may vary, but the same vital juice runs through them all. At the same time he held that all religions are imperfect, because truth comes to human beings through human channels. He thought that there was no point in tearing away a man from the natural surroundings of his own religion and putting him inside an alien religion.

He was against uprooting from anybody's mind, and especially from the minds of innocent and simple people, the faith in their respective religions. He deprecated the attempts of missionaries to change people's religions all of a sudden with no effective realization of the interplay between the individual and his cultural environment. For example, many Harijan ("untouchable") converts to Christianity became apathetic and morally and spiritually lost ground after having lost their "gods." He felt keenly about such conversions.

Gandhi's own approach to the subject was very different. He could no more think of asking a Christian or a Mussalman to change his religion than he could think of changing his own. As he explained, "Here is Miraben.[2] I would have her find all the spiritual comfort she needs from Christianity, and I should not dream of converting her to Hinduism, even if she wanted to do so. Today it is the case of a grown-up woman like her; tomorrow it may be that of a European child entrusted to my care by a friend. Take the case of Khan Saheb's daughter entrusted to my care by her father. I should jealously educate her in her own faith and should strive my utmost against her being lured away from it, even if ever she was so inclined. I have had the privilege of having children and grown-up persons of other faiths with me. I was thankful to find them better Christians, Mussalmans, Parsis, or Jews by their contact with me. ... Let my missionary friends remember that it was none but that most Christ-like of all Christians, Albert Schweitzer, who gave Christianity a unique interpretation when he himself resolved 'not to preach any more, not to lecture any more' but to bury himself in Equatorial Africa simply with a view to fulfill somewhat the debt that Europe owes to Africa."[3]

What is needed is that all of us should help one another to rise to higher heights of moral and spiritual life, potential in our respective religions. We are not to "wean out" anyone from his or her religious affiliation. Gandhi gave his considered opinion on conversion thus : "I believe that there is no such thing as conversion from one faith to another in the accepted sense of the term. It is a highly personal matter for the individual and his God. I may not have any design upon my neighbor as to his faith, which I must honor even as I honor my own. For I regard all the great religions as true, at any rate for the people professing them, as mine is true for me. ... And seeing that it takes all my resources in trying to bring my practice to the level of my faith and in preaching the same to my co-religionists, I do not dream of preaching to the followers of other faiths. 'Judge not lest you be judged' is a sound maxim for one's conduct. It is a conviction daily growing upon me that the great and rich Christian missions will render true service to India if they can persuade themselves to confine their activities to humanitarian service without the ulterior motive of converting India, or at least her unsophisticated villagers, to Christianity and destroying their social superstructure which notwithstanding its many defects has withstood from time immemorial the onslaughts on it from within and from without."[4]

Gandhi deprecated the offering of material advantages like money, educational facilities, and medical service to secure religious conversion. He thought conversions secured through secular aids to be degrading; he doubted whether they commanded the respect of and did honor to any religion. He observed, "I hold that proselytizing under the cloak of humanitarian work is, to say the least, unhealthy. It is most certainly resented by the people here. Religion, after all, is a deeply personal matter; it touches the heart. Why should I change my religion because a doctor who professes Christianity has cured me of some disease or why should the doctor expect or suggest such a change whilst I am under his influence ? Or why should I in a missionary educational institution have Christian teaching thrust upon me ? In my opinion, these practices are not uplifting and give rise to suspicion if not even secret hostility."[5] Elsewhere he observed, "Conversion and service go ill together."[6]

At the same time, Gandhi maintained that conversion in the sense of self-purification and self-realization was the crying need of our day. It is a normal need in humanity's moral development. This phenomenon occurs when people are made aware of a higher truth or universal value than that within which they are living, and at the same time become conscious that the higher value is one which they ought to reach. There is a crisis in their moral life, and life takes on a new aspect; the mind turns in criticism upon the life that is past. It is at such times that the inner life becomes prominent. But the modern methods of conversion rarely focus on the quality of inner life. "Conversion nowadays has become a matter of business. I remember having read a missionary report saying how much it cost per head to convert and then presenting a budget for 'the next harvest.' "[7] Further, Gandhi suggested : "Conversion should mean a definite giving up of the evil of the old, adoption of all the good of the new, and a scrupulous avoidance of everything evil in the new. Conversion should therefore mean a life of greater dedication to one's own country, greater surrender to God, and greater self purification."[8]

Gandhi maintained that religion is best propagated through the noble lives led by its followers; no other propaganda could match that. "To live the Gospel is the most effective way... most effective in the beginning, in the middle, and in the end. Preaching jars on me and makes no appeal to me, and I get suspicious of missionaries who preach; but I love those who never preach but live the life according to their lights. There lives are a silent and yet most effective testimony. Therefore I cannot say what to preach, but I can say that a life of service and uttermost simplicity is the best preaching. A rose does not need to preach. It simply spreads its fragrance. The fragrance is its own sermon. If it had human understanding and if it could engage a number of preachers, the preachers would not be able to sell more roses than the fragrance itself could do. The fragrance of religious and spiritual life is much finer and subtler than that of the rose."[9]

In the reformation of life one may draw inspiration from every available source. It is not necessary to discard one's own religion to benefit by the teachings of other great religions. "If a person wants to believe in the Bible let him say so; but why should he discard his own religion ? This proselytization will mean no peace in the world. Religion is a very personal matter. We should by living the life according to our lights share the best with one another, thus adding to the sum total of human effort to reach God."[10] Further, "It is tragic to see that religion is dragged down to the low level of crude materialism, to lure people into which the most cherished sentiments of millions of human beings are trodden underfoot."[11]

In the psychological sense, real conversion, or inner change of heart, with corresponding differences in outward ways of life, is recognized as the birth of true religion in man. But real conversion or rebirth in spirit takes place in the lives of very few persons. Without the wonderful blessing of conversion a God-centered life is impossible. When such a new life begins, there is a new quickening of the spirit, a stronger attachment to God, and a new discipline to strengthen one's life. It is the ineursion of purity; it is a new birth. He is the truly regenerate person who has been reborn and whose face is now turned towards God. Such alone realize God. "Except one is born anew, he cannot see the kingdom of God."[12] In such conversions, the ethical and spiritual life of the person concerned is raised to a higher level and the heart is uplifted. One begins a new life which establishes the kingdom of God in the heart, bringing the joy of spiritual fulfillment. To be born of the spirit is indeed the real conversion. In the words of Gandhi, "Real conversion springs from the heart and at the prompting of God, not of a stranger. The voice of God can always be distinguished from the voice of man."[13]

J. A. H. Murray's *A New English Dictionary* gives one of the meanings of conversion thus: "In the medieval church: Change from the secular to religious life; entering into monastic life." Conversion is from the Latin verb *convertere* meaning to turn or change. Hence conversion means turning about or changing. True conversion is an actual overturning of the inner life. It opens up a new vision to morality and spirituality. In the words of Evelyn Underhill, "Conversion then is the larger world consciousness now pressing on the individual consciousness. Often it breaks in suddenly and becomes a great new revelation. This is the first aspect of conversion; the person emerges from a smaller limited world of existence into a large world of being. His life becomes swallowed up in a larger whole."[14] Conversion in this sense within the context of one's own religion is the first necessity of our times. As a matter of fact, "Nothing wonderful will happen to the world if the entire mankind be converted to Hinduism, Christianity, Buddhism, or Islam or to any other religion. But assuredly something marvelous will happen if a dozen of men and women pierce the thick walls of the church, temple, synagogue, and realize the Truth."[15] A person with the infectious fervor of creative religion must first of all work with his own religious group to kindle the fire of spirituality among his co-religionists. But to force the belief in one's own prophet as the only savior on all others is unacceptable.

The Koran takes an evolutionary view of religion and recognizes a long line of prophets in every religion and nation. It does not ask anyone to give up his or her religion, but bids people to recapture and return to the pristine purity of the original messages given by the prophets. The Koran recognizes the essential, unity of the religions of mankind. It does not sanction any compulsion in religion. The Prophet Muhammad allowed the fullest freedom of conscience to all the peoples he had dealings with. Islam believes in conversion through the preaching of the Koran and the influences of saints; but it gives its sanction only to genuine and spontaneous conversion of the spirit and not to conversions from fear or greed of any kind. But one cannot help noticing the great gap that has existed in history between Islamic practice and the sublime teachings of the Koran. But the founders of religions cannot be made responsible for the excesses of a few fanatics.

Conversion programs of today lie directly in the path of religious harmony; they are exercising the minds of many thinking people over the world. There is a need to understand the urge behind such programs and to point out a way of reconciliation in this regard between different religions. Gandhi insisted that whatever is high and noble in any religious tradition should be accepted, and whatever separates man from man should be rejected.

But according to him, the changing of religious labels is unnecessary. What is needed is to recognize a family unity among all religions; they all point towards God. What religions are called upon to undertake at this time, when the world has become one, is an adventure in faith, a fuller sharing of the deepest and the best within them, in a joint endeavor to achieve a just and peaceful world order in the religious field as in others. This has now become the very condition not only of human welfare but of human survival.

## (ii) The Interpretation of Scriptures

Gandhi held that mere theoretical knowledge or booklearning, however important, is insufficient to lead a man to salvation and spiritual fulfillment. The trouble with many scholastics is that they try to find wisdom in knowing about life, instead of seeking it in proper living. It is not mere study of the scriptures, but the realization of the experience recorded there that is necessary. Gandhi said, "We often confuse spiritual knowledge with spiritual attainment. Spirituality is not a matter of knowing scriptures and engaging in philosophic discussions. It is a matter of heart culture, of unmeasurable strength. Fearlessness is the first requisite to spirituality. Cowards can never be moral."[1] Elsewhere, he wrote, "Divine knowledge is not borrowed from books. It has to be realized in oneself. Books are at best an aid, often even a hindrance."[2]

Ignorant and selfish people interpret the scriptures variously and start forming sects and parties. They split themselves into opposing camps — each claiming to be the sole repository of truth — and begin to make totalitarian claims. Fortunately, from time to time reformers and saints are born who uphold the spirit of the scriptures and dispel wrong notions and interpretations. They take us back to fundamentals; they dive deep into the ocean of scripture and bring out the pearls of truth and wisdom. Actually, only the enlightened can convey truth to others and communicate the meaning and spirit of a scriptural text. Gandhi held that a certain discipline is necessary in order to be able to rightly understand and interpret the scriptures. He observed, "Our *Rishis* made the startling discovery (and every day I feel more and more convinced of its truth) that sacred texts and inspired writings yield their truth only in proportion as one has advanced in the practice of *ahiṁsā* and Truth. The greater the realization of Truth and *ahiṁsā*, the greater the illumination."[3]

The object of scriptural knowledge is much the same in every tradition. Scriptures are regarded as channels of religious revelation. They are preserved and recited in order to transmit and reproduce a certain religious experience. But words, by themselves, are very imperfect means of communication and are often misunderstood and misinterpreted. Pride or erudition, therefore, may be an obstacle in God realization. Gandhi refused to cling to the literal word of scripture; but he accepted the essence or the central thrust of the various scriptures and saw only the good in all religions. He wrote, "I am not a literalist. Therefore, I try to understand the spirit of various scriptures of the world. I apply the test of Truth and *ahiṁsā* laid down by these very scriptures for interpretation. I reject what is inconsistent with the test and I appreciate all that is consistent with it."[4]

Gandhi was not prepared to accept social and other evils as sacrosanct though certain scriptures were quoted by some people to defend these evils. That is how he could fight for the uplift of Harijans ("untouchables"). In his own words, "For myself, I regard my study of and reverence for the Bible, the Koran, and the other scriptures to be wholly consistent with my claims to be a staunch *sanātani* (orthodox) Hindu. He is no *sanātani* Hindu who is narrow, bigoted, and considers evil to be good if it has the sanction of authority and is to be found supported in any Sanskrit book. I claim to be a staunch *sanātani* Hindu because, though I reject all that offends my moral sense, I find the Hindu scriptures to satisfy the needs of the soul. My respectful study of other scriptures has not abated my reverence for or my faith in the Hindu scriptures. They have indeed left their deep mark upon my understanding of the Hindu scriptures. They have enabled me to understand more clearly many an obscure passage in Hindu scriptures."[5]

The goodness or otherwise of actions is not decided by quoting scripture. Gandhi had his own test: "Whatever falls from Truth should be rejected, no matter where it comes from; therefore the burden lies on the shoulders of that person who upholds a practice which is inconsistent with Truth; so that if a man wants to defend, for instance, untouchability, he has to show that it is consistent with Truth. Unless he shows that, all the authorities that he may cite in support of it are irrelevant."[6]

The ideas of an earlier age, as they are, cannot answer problems of all times. Our thinking ought to advance with the change of environments and change of times. The great leaders of all religions have been persons of great mobility and ceaseless adventure. They were men of originality and were not tied by old traditions. We should take our cue from them. We should understand the context of scriptural statements; only then can we understand their sense. Further, the genius of the spiritual leader is not independent of his age and circumstances. Though the living spiritual force is within him, the conditions of its development are without and around him. Therefore fresh interpretations of scripture become necessary to suit new times and conditions. We shall be disloyal to the very spirit of the great religious teachers if we go on repeating old and worn-out formulas in a world of perpetual movement and change.

When certain orthodox brahmins objected to the imparting of the Vedas to *śūdras* on the authority of scriptural sanction, Gandhi answered : "The story of a *śūdra* having been punished by Rāmachandra for daring to learn the Veda, I reject as an interpolation. And in any event, I worship Rāma, the perfect being of my conception, not a historical person the facts about whose life may vary with the progress of new historical discoveries and researches. Tulsidas had nothing to do with the Rāma of history. Judged by historical facts, his *Rāmāyaṇa* would be fit for a scrap heap. As a spiritual experience, his book is almost unrivaled, at least for me. And then too, I do not swear by every word that is to be found in so many editions published as the book of *Rāmāyaṇa* of Tulsidas. It is the spirit running through the book that holds me spell-bound. I cannot myself subscribe to the prohibition against *śūdras* learning Vedas. Indeed, in my opinion at the present moment, we are predominantly *śūdras* as long as we are serfs. Knowledge cannot be the prerogative of any class or section. But I can conceive the impossibility of people assimilating higher or subtler truths unless they have undergone preliminary training, even as those who have not made preliminary preparations are quite unfit to breathe the rarefied atmosphere in high altitudes, or those who have no preliminary training in simple mathematics are unfit to understand or assimilate higher geometry or algebra."[7]

When a man has an open mind, he is logically bound to make use of reason fully and welcome truth from whatever source it might come. Gandhi rejected the claim of any ancient scripture to unquestioning acceptance, whether Hindu, Muslim, Christian, or any other. He said, "I shall not make a fetish of religion and I cannot justify any evil in its sacred name. I have no desire to carry one single soul with me if I cannot convince him by an appeal to reason." He further maintained that a seeker of Truth should sacrifice not merely all his material belongings but should shed his prejudices and pet theories. Unless one is not purged of all preconceptions one cannot hope to attain Truth, and a great deal of self-analysis and discrimination is necessary to accomplish this result. He gave his considered opinion on the question thus : "The seat of religious authority lies within. I exercise my judgment about every scripture including the Gītā. I cannot let a scriptural text supersede my reason. Whilst I believe that the principal books are inspired, they suffer from a process of double distillation. Firstly, they come through a human prophet, and then through the commentaries of interpreters. Nothing in them comes from God directly. Matthew may give one version of one text and John may give another. I cannot surrender my reason while I subscribe to divine revelation. And above all, 'the letter killeth, the spirit giveth life' (2 Cor. 3:6)."[8]

### (iii) The Wheat and the Chaff

Organized religions are aids to the spiritual and moral development of those who believe in them. They come into being because of the need to translate eternal and universal truths for particular societies in space and time. Though these essential and universal truths are valid for all times and conditions, they have to be made accessible to particular communities. Different communities have different languages and different social and cultural environments, and every society is in its own particular stage of intellectual and cultural development. All these factors condition the expression of the eternal and universal truths. In the words of Arnold Toynbee, "These accidental accretions are the price that the permanently and universally valid essence of a higher religion has to pay for communicating its message to the members of a particular society's history. ... The price of redemption is incarnation."[1]

It must also be recognized that a considerable watering down of the founder's teaching (in every religion) takes place to accommodate it to the needs of the masses. It is of fundamental importance to distinguish the essential truths of a religion from the merely local and temporary. If one cannot do so, there is danger of adhering to the incidental and the temporary elements and neglecting the essentials. Let us take for instance the teachings of the New Testament. Here we must remember that Jesus was talking at a particular time in history to particular audiences. He was not talking to humanity in general. He was in the midst of a very serious conflict; he was persecuted by men who were determined to get rid of him and his "dangerous" teaching. This does not mean that the statements of Jesus are not filled with eternal truth: they are, of course. But we shall miss that truth if we think it is contained only in the literal statements of the New Testament. These statements are not just words of wisdom; they are the records of what were essentially actions; what Jesus did when people attacked him or sought his help. They indicate how he responded. His whole personality and an awareness of the whole situation lay behind the words, and conditioned them. We must recreate the situation for ourselves in imagination in order to know what his teachings mean. As Toynbee says: "The true purpose of a higher religion is to radiate the spiritual counsels and truths that are its essence into as many souls as it can reach in order that each of these souls may be enabled thereby to fulfill the true end of man. Man's true end is to glorify God and to enjoy Him for ever; and if the ecclesiastical authorities were to make this true purpose of their religion the paramount consideration in the determination of their policy, they should constantly be returning their unvarying essential message to different wave-lengths in order to make it audible to different audiences."[2]

Unfortunately, not all religions have made such attempts, and therefore more often than not they have clashed with one another on very flimsy and unimportant matters — unimportant from a spiritual point of view. Self-preservation often appears to have become their primary concern. The original sin of religions seems to be to objectify the Divine and to accept as final some particular dogmas, sacraments, or rituals. This sort of enforced uniformity will sooner or later give rise to new and unexpected interpretations suited to altered circumstances. It is only a sincere and a steady introspection that can show us whether we are within the permissible limits of spiritual truth or are being driven beyond them by blind attachment to creeds and dogmas. According to Toynbee, "They (Religious believers) are apt to make the preservation of their church their paramount aim; and this consideration tempts them to insist that their religious heritage must be treated as an indivisible whole, in which the accidental accretions are to be accepted as being not less sacrosanct than the essence itself; they are moved to this line by two fears. They are afraid of distressing and eliminating the weaker brethren, and they are afraid that, if once they admit that any element in the heritage is local and temporary and therefore discardable, they may find themselves unable to draw a line or make a stand anywhere till the very essence of religion is surrendered. ... But such a policy is wrong; it is bad psychology and bad statemanship."[3]

It is due to the lack of such a sifting process that the history of religion has witnessed the sad story of jehads, crusades, inquisitions, and persecutions. The tragedy is that different religions which try to understand the one eternal Truth should deem it necessary to wage war against one another, instead of cooperating together to unravel the great mystery within and around us.

Religions that hold the conviction that they are completed systems that have been revealed once and for all, are liable sooner or later to become unsatisfactory to intelligent believers. Many details that are thought to be essential to religion do not derive from the founders of the religions concerned, but from the centuries that follow. Such a mass statement of doctrine may contain elements of eternal significance, but it also as surely reflects the peculiar needs and habits of the historical period concerned. These needs and habits change from time to time. For instance, rituals and doctrines that were meaningful in the first few centuries after Buddha or Christ may not be wholly adequate to the life of the people of the 20th century. To ensure that our religion is adequate to present needs, we have to break with all the useless accretions that have obscured its inner worth and significance. We have to cut away these excrescences and remember afresh the core of the ancient wisdom. We have to get out of obsolete ways of thought and living. We have to frequently focus our attention on a religion's highest teaching and reform what is not essential.

That is what Gandhi did for Hinduism. Hinduism after Gandhi is not the same as it was before him. It has been reformed and rejuvenated. He mercilessly rejected many old, meaningless, and harmful practices, upholding the ancient wisdom of Hinduism and making it serve and suit the needs and circumstances of our own times. This kind of reinterpretation is needed in all the religions. As a result of it, the wisdom and truths contained in all religions will shine and the accidental accretions will be relegated to subsidiary levels — where they belong.

**References**

(i) The Problem of Conversion

1. *Harijan*, 17-1-1937.
2. An English woman who became a disciple of Gandhi and who wanted at one time to become a Hindu.
3. *Harijan*, 25-1-1935.
4. *Ibid.*, 28-9-1935.
5. *Young India*, 23-4-1931.
6. *Ibid.*, 19-1-1928.
7. *Ibid.*, 23-4-1931.
8. *Ibid.*, 20-8-1925.
9. *Harijan*, 29-3-1935.
10. *Young India*, 23-9-1926.
11. *Harijan*, 8-8-1936.
12. John 3 : 3.
13. *Harijan*, 25-9-1937.
14. Underhill, E., *Mysticism*, Meridian Books, New York, 1960, p. 214.
15. Swami Nikhilananda, *The Māṇḍūkya Upanishad with Gauḍapāda's Kārikā*, Sri Ramakrishna Math, Mysore, p. xxxv.

(ii) The Interpretation of Scriptures

1. *Young India*, 13-10-1921.
2. *Ibid.*, 17-2-1924.
3. *Ibid.*, 29-1-1925.
4. *Ibid.*, 27-8-1925.
5. *Ibid.*, 2-9-1926.
6. *Ibid.*, 29-9-1927.
7. *Ibid.*, 27-8-1925.
8. *Harijan*, 5-12-1936.

(iii) The Wheat and the Chaff

1. Arnold Toynbee, *An Historian's Approach to Religion*, Oxford University Press, New York, 1956, p. 264.
2. *Ibid.*, p. 266.
3. *Ibid.*, p. 266.

CHAPTER 6

# CONCLUSIONS

GANDHI'S comparative study of religions made it clear to him that a mere doctrinaire approach in order to promote one's own faith may not be sufficient to bring about genuine understanding of other religions and much less to bring about inter-religious fellowship. No creative dialogue is possible among dogmatic religions, because they all make claims which are virtually totalitarian. The religious dogmas of each of these religions induce directly or indirectly an attitude of apathy if not contempt towards the dogmas of other religions. "If religion concerns itself with peculiar historical events, there is not much meeting ground among followers of different religions, who adopt different historical events as their religious-bases."[1] Fanatics of one religion insist that the followers of other religions are mistaken and that their only chance of salvation lies in accepting the one true religion. Even when they are confronted by values they cannot deny in other religions, they make the subtle claim that these values are merely approximations of what they hold sacred in their own particular religion, thus preparing a way for a fuller and final acceptance by them of the one complete religion. They refuse, of course, to grant that there is anything lacking in their own faith. Such being the case, they hardly find opportunities of fellowship with the followers of other religions. The result is the perpetuation of prejudice. Hence arises the need to approach religions in terms of the inner life of men and women, rather than of the forms the religions assume. This is a viable way of inter-religious understanding and fellowship.

Religion, properly understood, vitalizes and elevates the inner life of human beings. Organized religions should be able to activate the inner spiritual life of their followers so that it may express itself in universal dimensions. From this point of view, the religiousness of a person depends not on professions or subscriptions, but on the application of the tenets of one's faith to one's day-to-day life. If organized religions, through any of their agencies, hamper the growth of the inner life, then the very purpose of religion is defeated. The church, the mosque, the temple, and all the rituals and symbols of religion are helpful only so long as they nourish and fertilize the inner spiritual life of their respective followers.

Gandhi pointed out that the salvation of the world can only come through a resurgence of moral and religious values which are eternal. He did an inestimable service to humanity by stressing the importance and purity of means even where the ends are noble. He motivated members of different religions to cooperate in various fields of social and moral reconstruction. He chalked out programs of action whose aim was to create good will, mutual respect, and inter-religious harmony. To him work was worship. All work done selflessly and for uplifting the oppressed and the downtrodden is work that speaks of the glory of God. The social service schemes started by Gandhi — such as Harijan welfare, village reconstruction, basic education, etc.— were of this type. He called upon the religious leaders of the world to an adventure of faith, to a full sharing of the deepest and best within their heritage with others in a joint endeavor to achieve a just and peaceful world order — perhaps the only condition of human survival. The life of the Buddha and Zoroaster and Christ and Muhammad, and the teachings of Vedānta, should furnish the spiritual background for humanity's search for a better life on this earth and beyond.

The primary task of all religions is to awaken the spiritual consciousness of humanity and to bring to the surface the forces of love, sacrifice, service, self-control, and above all, devotion to truth and righteousness. The great religions can and ought to cooperate in promoting and propagating the good life for all. In every society there are social and moral evils. Religions should join hands in rooting out these evils, for the resources of all religions are needed to eradicate the evils in human society. It is the duty of all religious-minded people not to stand apart in their differences, but to stand together and work for the greater glory of God and the greater happiness of mankind. We cannot treat religions in isolation from one another. In their higher aspects, all religions call for peace and brotherhood among all people. The religions, therefore, working singly and together, should spiritualize all human activities.

In order to encourage the understanding and appreciation of the different religions, a fresh and creative type of religious education is necessary. The religions should be presented at their best without creating any kind of prejudice against any particular religion. The emphasis should be on the cultivation of appreciation for and understanding of the valuable insights throughout the religious history of mankind. It is sad that though, in general, men and women do not have an adequate knowledge of their own religion, they are yet ready to throw stones at those of others. Once Gandhi complained, "From my sixth and seventh year and up to my sixteenth, I was at school, being taught all sorts of things except religion. I may say that I failed to get from the teachers what they could have given me without any effort on their part. And yet I kept on picking up things here and there from my surroundings."[2] Non-sectarian religious instruction must be introduced in schools where there are students belonging to different religions. When educational institutions thus take up the teachings of religions, the students are likely to imbibe a more liberal type of religion than they do in sectarian seminaries. As a matter of fact, the child is robbed of its full development if it receives no guidance in early years towards a recognition of the religious aspect of life. If this guidance is left to homes and communities, the chances are that communal bigotry, intolerance, and selfishness may increase.

Young men and women, whether they are Hindus, Buddhists, Jews, Christians, or Muslims, must be taught their own religion in an enlightened manner, so that they may all love one another and may know that God is one for all. They should feel that they are all of the one great family of human beings. It should produce in each a reverent consciousness of a transcendent and benevolent power, irrespective of the individual approaches to that power in varying forms of worship. It should develop a sense of genuine acceptance of different forms of worship. In short, they should be helped to see that all sincere religious persons are fellow pilgrims marching towards the spiritual realization of Truth and love.

Much of the mutual unfriendliness that sometimes characterizes inter-religious relations arises out of a sense of strangeness and unfamiliarity with one another's faith. There is a tendency in human beings to dislike the unfamiliar. For example, words like *heathen*, *idolatry*, *superstition*, *kaffir*, *mlechha*, are often used in derision with reference to other religions and are never applied to one's own religion or religious practices. Even though persons belonging to different religious groups and cultural traditions live as neighbors, they live more often than not in their own separate worlds. No points of contact exist on the deeper levels of religious and cultural life. It is possible for people to be near neighbors all their lives without quarreling, but also without even knowing one another in genuine friendship. Though they are neighbors physically, they continue to be strangers at heart, because the one does not sympathetically know the other in his cultural life and religious faith.

In his own life, Gandhi tried to bridge this cultural distance by "community living," where persons of different religions, cultures, and races came to live and work together for common ends. The sense of a common purpose helps bridge the gulf of prejudice, custom, creed, and culture. He recommended the *āshram* type of community living, or even community living in camps for brief periods of time; it provides opportunities for the sharing of ideas and communication of heart to heart. The members share problems, cooperate mutually towards their solutions, understand one another through thick and thin, and realize that in spite of all diversities they are all human beings. In this universal human context, they are given an opportunity to realize their unity, and transcend all those things by which humanity is divided. In approximating this ideal, they prove that despite differences of caste, creed, and race, they are all one family under God. The common sharing of joys and sorrows welds members of such a community into oneness, sensitive sympathy, and mutual understanding.

There are those who find in different religions many resemblances and in a fundamental sense an underlying unity among them. Such people should come together and work out acceptable common programs of study, prayer, and service. Open and free discussions with a view to understanding others' points of view should be encouraged; these provide the best opportunity and environment to enable persons to appreciate the varied meanings and rich implications of each other's scriptures. In the words of Gandhi, "Unless and until we realize this fundamental unity, wars in the name of religion will not cease. These are not confined to Hindus and Mussalmans alone. The pages of world history are soiled with the bloody accounts of these religious wars. Religion can be defended only by the purity of its adherents and their good deeds, never by their quarrels with those of other faiths."[3]

When followers of different religions meet with one another in this spirit, though at first there may be some apprehension, in the long run good results are bound to follow for all. The life of Gandhi is a superb example of the whole-some results that flow from the interaction of different religions. The personality of Gandhi, his stature and his universality of outlook, are the result of the influence of many religions and cultures. His philosophical outlook was shaped by the teachings of Christianity, Islam, Buddhism, Zoroastrianism, and other faiths, even while his roots were in Hinduism. Actually, no single religion can claim exclusive credit for the flowering of Gandhi's personality.

Since spirituality is inherent in all peoples and cultures, the meeting of religions can only be a blessing to them. For it will remind them of forgotten or neglected dimensions of their own tradition. Further, it will challenge every religion to revive its own undeveloped resources and discover new spiritual horizons. For example, the advent of Christianity in the eighteenth and nineteenth centuries had a considerable effect in India and South East Asia in stimulating the religious quest. It made more explicit the need for reform in Hindu and Buddhist societies. The religious leaders realized their duty towards the poor and the downtrodden. On the other hand, Christianity and Islam in India have become less fanatical and more introspective because of the impact of Hinduism. Even differences often prove helpful, provided those involved are tolerant, charitable, and truthful. Gandhi saw around him an overemphasis on individual salvation in religion to the neglect of service to humanity. Spiritual life was divorced from practical life, and the two were considered mutually inconsistent. Therefore, Gandhi was never tired of pointing out to his countrymen that spirituality did not consist in turning away from poverty, ignorance, and misery in the world, but in fully facing and fighting them. As a result of his teaching, there has come a rejuvenation of the spiritual life of the Indian people. He interpreted his own religion in the light of the teachings of other religions and the progress of knowledge, thus enabling Hinduism to survive and progress.

An ideal religious life would mean a true synthesis of science and spirituality, of knowledge and faith pointing the direction towards the realization of the good life for all. The whole world is physically united by science. It is inevitable that in the long run this fact will bring about more mutual knowledge and human sympathy. Appreciation follows understanding. Further knowledge, if it is to be adequate, must take into account not merely the physical universe, but also the universal emotions of love, holiness, affection, of the longing for perfection, and so on, all of which characterize the human soul and provide the driving force for human progress.

Science without spirituality is amoral. J. B. S. Haldane observes, "The conclusion forced upon me in the course of a life devoted to natural science is that the universe as it is assumed to be in physical science is only an idealized world, while the real universe is the spiritual universe in which spiritual values count for everything."[4] There cannot be any antagonism between true science and true religion. The truths of science and the truths of religion can no more contradict each other than God can contradict Himself. All truths stream from the same fountainhead and, when properly understood, must harmonize with one another. To quote Haldane again, "The advance of scientific knowledge does not seem to make either our universe or our inner life in it any less mysterious."[5]

No single religion, however, has ever or can ever unite humanity, only the underlying spirituality of all religions can unite the whole human race. This goal will be realized when science is allied to spirituality and when religion is rid of dogmatism. Science and religion will have both lived in vain if men and women fail to realize that both deal with the same living, breathing Reality. The scientific outlook should therefore be applied in the religious field, and, in turn, science must become tempered by religion. Then what is essential will remain and superficial things will automatically drop away. Is there any religion higher than Truth and any practice higher than love ? Is not this a sufficient basis for mutual cooperation, one that can be discovered in all religions?

To carry universal conviction, any idea we wish to convey should have unity with the spirit of humanity. Anything that divides humanity is evil. Religions should operate as life and spirit, not merely as doctrine and dogma. True religion implies a warmth of heart that goes out to human misery wherever it is. When this spirit permeates all religions, sectarian pride and fanaticism must fade away. There is no link so potent as the spiritual to bind humanity together and lead to its goal. Along with the synthesis of the scientific and the spiritual outlook, there is a further advantage in the meeting of religions. As a result, each tradition should be able to remove its own harmful historical accretions and learn from all the others.

It is one thing to talk about religious toleration; it is another and a much better thing to practice brotherly love to the neighbor of another faith. According to Gandhi, what a man *does*, and not what he *preaches*, is important. In the realm of religion we can *know* only as we truly *participate*. Professor Sorokin writes, "If Christianity and its norms of conduct as they are enunciated in the Sermon on the Mount were really practiced by Christians, and if Confucianism and Taoism, Hinduism and Buddhism, Judaism and Jainism, Mohammedanism and other religions, with their moral commandments were actually realized in the 'overt' behavior of their followers, then they would exert a decisive influence upon the inhibition of war. Through the universal practice of love, all hatred, antagonism, and injustice would be eliminated and abiding harmony would prevail throughout the entire human universe. ... Unfortunately there has been a vast discrepancy between what the followers of all these religions have preached and what they have practiced."[6] Sorokin adds : "Religion must be vitalized by all-giving and forgiving love; love of man for his fellow men, for God, and for the entire universe, love manifest in deeds as well as in words and aspirations. ...and it must inspire man with an unquenchable longing to transcend the subconscious and conscious phases of his personality, in quest of the superconscious realm of immortal truth, goodness, and beauty."[7]

Truth is one and indivisible, common to all human beings, all religions and philosophies. No doubt the truths of religions are enduring; but more often than not, these truths become associated and confused with the worldly hopes and aspirations of their respective followers. Every religion undergoes a process of growth and evolution as long as it is a dynamic force. And the eternal truths have to be correlated to the growing scientific and social thoughts of the times and reinterpreted and worked into ever fresh systems of philosophy. That is what the Buddha did for Hinduism, and Jesus did for Judaism. That is what Gandhi did for Hinduism in the 20th century. Every religion brings into relief one or more aspects of Truth; it is therefore no use engaging in religious conflicts. As Sorokin observes, "The dominant religions and denominations must cease their 'imperialistic' struggle for superiority and 'vested interests,' laying aside their rivalry, they must stress their common basic verities and their common moral imperatives."[8] Further, "Like different languages, each denoting the same objects in its own words and idioms, humanity may have different 'religious languages' each in its own way conveying the experience of the Holy, putting men in touch with the Infinite Manifold, and constituting the indispensable creativity of their culture and of a peaceful, altruistic social system."[9]

The world does not need a new religion. What it does need is a greater number of men and women who, discovering the universal truths in their own traditions, will dare to live in accordance with them. When they do so, all the dry externals of the different religious systems which today divide human from human will inevitably crumble before the radiance of the renewed human spirit which has never yet been vanquished in all recorded history. Nothing is more potent or surcharged with greater power than the human soul, and if religion is its vehicle, then that vehicle will be transformed, again and again, as the soul advances increasingly towards participation in the life of the Divine Being.

**References**

CONCLUSIONS

1. *The Report of the University Education Commission*, Vol. 1, p. 298. vide ante.
2. M. K. Gandhi, *An Autobiography*, p. 31.
3. *Harijan*, 13-7-1940.

4. Haldane, J. B. S., *Science and Philosophy*, p. 273.
5. *Ibid.*, p. 165.
6. Sorokin, P., *Reconstruction of Humanity*, The Beacon Press, 1948, p. 41.
7. *Ibid.*, p. 115.
8. *Ibid.*, p. 115.
9. *Ibid.*, p. 117.

## SELECT BIBLIOGRAPHY


Andrews, C. F., *Mahatma Gandhi's Ideas*, Macmillan Company, 1930.

Andrews, C. F., *Mahatma Gandhi at Work*, Macmillan Company, 1931.

Bondurant, Joan, Conquest of Violence, Princeton University, 1958.

Datta, D. M., *Philosophy of Mahatma Gandhi*, The University of Wisconsin Press.

Desai, V. G., tr. *From Yeravda Mandir*, Navajivan, Ahmedabad, Navajivan, 1932.

Dhavan, Gopinath, *The Political Philosophy of Mahatma Gandhi*, Navajivan, 1952.

Diwakar, R. R., *Satyagraha, the Power of Truth*, Hinsdale, Illinois, Henry Regnery Company, 1948.

Erikson, Erik H., *Gandhi's Truth*, Norton & Co., New York. 1969

Fischer, Louis, *The Life of Mahatma Gandhi*, Harper & Brothers, New York, 1950.

Gandhi, M. K., *An Autobiography*, Beacon Press, Boston, 1957.

Gandhi, M. K., *Communal Unity*, Navajivan Publishing House, Ahmedabad, 1949.

Gandhi, M. K., *Hindu Dharma*, Navajivan Publishing House, Ahmedabad, 1949.

Gandhi, M. K., *My Religion*, Navajivan Publishing House, Ahmedabad.

Gandhi, M. K., *The Collected Works of Mahatma Gandhi*, Ministry of Information and Broadcasting, Government of India, Navajivan, 1958.

Gandhi, M. K., *The Removal of Untouchability*, Navajivan Publishing House, 1954.

Greg, Richard, *The Power of Non-Violence*, Schocken Books, New York, 1970.

Holmes, J. H., *My Gandhi*, Harper Bros., 1953.

Hoyland, J. S., *The Cross Moves East*, Allen and Unwin, London, 1931.

Hussain, S. Abid, *The Way of Gandhi and Nehru*, Asia Publishing House, London, 1959.

Issacs, Harold, *India's Ex-Untouchables*, John Day and Co., New York, 1960.

Jack, Homer A., *Gandhi Reader*, Indiana University Press, 1962.

Kumarappa, B., ed., *Christian Missions, Their Place in India*, Navajivan Publishing House, 1957.

Majumdar, H. T., *Mahatma Gandhi : Peaceful Revolutionary*, Navajivan Press, 1952.

Manshardt, Clifford, ed., *Mahatma and the Missionary*, Chicago, Henry Regnery, 1949.

Mashruwala, *Gandhi and Marx*, Navajivan Publishing House.

Naera, Anne, *Gandhi and the Nuclear Age*, The Westminster Press, 1965.

Nanda, B. R., *Mahatma Gandhi*, Harper, New York, 1950.

Nehru, Jawaharlal, *Nehru on Gandhi*, John Day and Co., New York, 1948.

Polak, H. S. L., *Mahtma Gandhi*, H. N. Brailsford & Lord Pethick-Lawrence, London, Odhams Press, 1949.

Prabhu, R. K., ed., *Truth is God*, Navajivan Publishing House, 1957.

Pyarelal, *Mahatma Gandhi—The Last Phase*, 2 vols. Navajivan, Ahmedabad, 1958.

Ramaiyer, A., *Ethical Religion*, M. K. Gandhi, Ganesan & Co., Madras, 1921.

Rolland, Romain, *Mahtma Gandhi*, Allen and Unwin, London, 1924.

Sheean, Vincent, *Lead, Kindly Light*, Random House, New York, 1949.

Tendulkar, D. G., *Mahatma : Life of Mohandas Karaumchand Gandhi*, 8 vols. V. K. Jhaveri and D. G. Tendulkar, 1951-54.

## *Journals*

*Indian Opinion*, Natal, South Africa (1903-1914)

*Young India*, Ahmedabad, India (1919-1932)

*Harijan*, Ahmedabad, India (1933-1948)

INDEX